Emma Albani

Victorian Diva
by Cheryl MacDonald

Dundurn Press Limited
Toronto and London
1984

Editor: Bernice Lever
Design and production: Ron and Ron Design Photography
Front cover illustration: Brenda Clark
Typesetting: Trans Canada Graphics
Printing: Marquis Printing, Montmagny, Quebec

The publication of this book was made possible by support from several sources. The author and publisher wish to acknowledge the generous assistance and ongoing support of the Canada Council and the Ontario Arts Council.

J. Kirk Howard, Publisher

Published by
Dundurn Press Limited
P.O. Box 245, Station F
Toronto, Canada
M4Y 2L5

Canadian Cataloguing in Publication Data
MacDonald, Cheryl Emily, 1952-
  Emma Albani : Victorian diva

(Dundurn lives ; 1)
Bibliography: p.
Includes index.
ISBN 0-919670-75-X (bound) — 0-919670-74-1 (pbk.)

1. Albani, Emma, Dame.   2. Singers — Canada —
Biography.   I. Title.   II. Series.

ML420.A5M24   1984   782.1′092′4   C84-098932-6

Emma Albani

Victorian Diva

ALBANI.

A nineteenth century magazine illustration of Emma Albani.

Contents

List of Illustrations and Photographs 7

Preface 8

Works Mme Albani Performed 13

1. A Difficult Childhood 19
2. Sisters of Sacré-Coeur 27
3. Albany Years 34
4. Singing Lessons in Paris 38
5. Sicilian Debut 46
6. Contract at Covent Garden 57
7. A Promising Prima Donna 65
8. An Engagement in Russia 77
9. First American Tour 84
10. Oratorio and Arthur Sullivan 91
11. Home, Sweet Home 104
12. Emma and Wagnerian Opera 114
13. Grande Dame of British Opera 124
14. Concerts in Canada 131
15. American Touring Company 139
16. Mexican Tour and New York Met 149
17. Touring the British Empire 161
18. Favourite of Queen Victoria 169
19. The Final Act 181

Afterword 187

Chronology 189

Notes 193

Bibliography 199

Illustration and Photograph Credits 203

Index 204

List of Illustrations and Photographs

Emma Albani, an etching 4
Magazine illustration of her most famous roles 12
Lajeunesse Family Tree 17
Emma Albani at five 18
A sketch of her Chambly home 22
A young Emma Albani 37
Emma Albani at her debut in Messina 45
Emma Albani in England 50
Covent Garden: exterior and interior views 56
Sir Frederick Gye, manager of Covent Garden 59
The Royal Box at Covent Garden in 1863 66
Adelina Patti, Spanish prima donna 74
Emma Albani in the role of Linda 76
Charles Gounod and his note 97
Sir Arthur Sullivan 99
Jean de Reszke, the Polish tenor 120
Johannes Brahms 128
Luigi Arditi, conductor 138
Francesco Tamagno, the Italian tenor 143
Emma Albani in the role of Marguerite 155
The New Grand Opera House, Toronto 157
Emma Albani wearing her pearl cross
   and decorations 160
A mature Emma Albani on tour 167
Queen Victoria 170
A letter from Queen Victoria 175
Emma Albani and music from the Messiah .. 180
Emma Albani's medals and decorations 182

Preface

She was Canada's first international celebrity, a convent-educated French-Canadian girl from Chambly who rose to prominence as one of the best operatic sopranos of the nineteenth century. This seems an almost miraculous achievement because opera was dominated by Europeans, particularly the Italians, French and Germans, who had long operatic traditions. No such tradition existed in Canada or in the United States, where Emma spent her early years. Yet, on closer examination, it is obvious her success was no miracle but the result of hard work and unswerving belief in her own capabilities.

To understand the scope of Emma's achievement, it is necessary to understand the status of opera in the nineteenth century. A century ago there were no such electronic diversions. You either made your own entertainment, alone or with friends, or sought it in live performances of which opera had the most influence. The elements it incorporated: well-known, often well-loved stories, drama, stirring music, magnificent sets and costumes, made it universally appealing. Moreover, the opera stars themselves were a major attraction, and they sparked a lively curiosity in their audiences. Their indiscretions, love affairs, professional rivalries and personal foibles were followed as closely as those of any celebrity. Opera was a colourful, dramatic world, at least from the outside, and Emma Albani was an important part of it.

Honoured by monarchs as diverse as Nicholas II of Russia, Queen Victoria of England and the King of Hawaii, she performed for the most prominent people of the Victorian age. She met Sir John A. Macdonald, Sir Wilfrid Laurier, Empress Eugénie of France, Lord Kitchener and U.S. President Chester Arthur, as well as scores of other notables. Her musical colleagues included Liszt, Gounod, Ambroise Thomas, Sir Arthur Sullivan and Nellie Melba. Many of the finest musicians of the time were happy to be her friend. Emma not only charmed everyone with her graciousness, but also she won respect from her colleagues with her dedicated professionalism. She was so highly thought of, in fact, that several nations competed for the honour of calling her their own. One newspaper reporter wrote, "What an elastic nationality she possessed. In America, she was an American and hailed from Albany. In England, she was declared to be a Canadian and a loyal subject of her British majesty. The French papers now state she is a Frenchwoman, her real name being Lajeunesse."[1]

Emma Albani's career was exceptional. Her story explains why she was the most respected and best loved of all the international divas of the Victorian era.

Cheryl MacDonald

December 1983

To Mum and Dad
With Love

Acknowledgements

So many people have assisted in the preparation of this book that it would be impossible to express my appreciation to each one individually. There are some, however, who deserve special mention: Sisters Archambault and Déry of Sacré-Coeur Convent in Montreal; Bernadette Laflamme of the Chambly Historical Society; Claire Messier, who located invaluable reference sources for me on a visit to Fort Chambly; Richard W. Ward of the Clinton County (New York) Historical Society and Clinton-Essex-Franklin Library System, who found Albani scrapbooks for me on extremely short notice, and his assistant, Tim Harnett; Kathleen M. Toomey of McGill University Library in Montreal; countless other librarians in Hamilton and Albany, and especially Joyce Lindsay and her staff at Selkirk Library (City of Nanticoke) who patiently ordered dozens of books on interlibrary loan for me. I must also express my gratitude to my sister, Sandra MacDonald; Kirk Howard, my publisher; and Bernice Lever, my editor; the Ontario Arts Council for their support and encouragement. Finally, extra special thanks to my mother, Margaret MacDonald, who acted as chauffeur and research assistant in Montreal, Chambly, Plattsburgh, Albany, and Ottawa, and who has actively encouraged me to write since childhood.

Sketches of her most famous roles along with her son, and with sprays of maple leaves to suggest her birthplace: Canada

Works Emma Albani Performed

Operatic roles sung by Emma Albani during her career, between 1869 and 1896. The name of the composers is followed by that of the role, the operas, the city and year of Albani's first performance. Compiled by Gilles Potvin, 1984©

Auber	**Les Diamants de la Couronne**	Catherine	London, 1873
Bellini	**I Puritani**	Elvira	London, 1874
	La Sonnambula	Amina	Messina, 1869
	Norma	Norma	Paris, 1877
Boito	**Mefistofele**	Margherita	London, 1882
		Elena	London, 1882
Cowen, F.	**Harold or The Norman Conquest***	Edith	London, 1895
Donizetti	**La Regina di Golconda**	Alina	Messina, 1870
	Lucia di Lammermoor	Lucia	Malta, 1870
	Linda di Chamounix	Linda	London, 1872
Flotow	**Martha**	Lady Harriet	London, 1872
	Alma l'incantatrice	Alma	Paris, 1878
Glinka	**La Vita per lo Czar**	Antonida	London, 1887
Gluck	**Iphigenia in Tauris** **(concert performance)**	Iphigenia	Liverpool, 1888
Gounod	**Faust**	Marguerite	London, 1875
	Roméo et Juliette*	Juliette	Antwerp, 1884
Hérold	**Le pré-aux-clercs**	Isabelle	London, 1880
Massé	**Paul et Virginie**	Virginie	London, 1878
Massenet	**Le Roi de Lahore**	Sita	London, 1880 ?
Meyerbeer	**L'Africana**	Inez	Malta, 1870
	Roberto il Diavolo	Isabella	Malta, 1870
	Les Huguenots	Valentine	London, 1890
Mozart	**Don Giovanni**	Zerlina	Paris, 1877
		Donna Elvira	New York, 1892
		Donna Anna	London, 1896
	Le Nozze di Figaro	Contessa	London, 1875
Reyer	**Sigurd**	Bruenhilde	Paris, 1884
Romani	**Il Mantello**	Giulietta	Malta, 1871
Rossini	**Il Barbiere di Siviglia**	Rosina	Malta, 1870
	Le Comte Ory	Adèle	Florence, 1872
Rubinstein, A.	**Il Demonio***	Tamara	London, 1881
Thomas	**Mignon**	Mignon	Florence, 1872
	Hamlet	Ofelia	London, 1873

Verdi	Un Ballo in Maschera	Oscar	Messina, 1869
	Rigoletto	Gilda	Cento, 1870
	Ernani	Elvira	Paris, 1878
	La Traviata	Violetta	Paris, 1878
	Otello	Desdemona	Chicago, 1890
Wagner	Lohengrin	Elsa	New York, 1874
	Tannhauser	Elisabeth	London, 1876
	Il Vascello Fantasma	Senta	London, 1877
	Die Meistersinger	Eva	London, 1889
	Tristan und Isolde	Isolde	London, 1896

*Sung under the direction of the composer

Oratorios, cantatas and other major vocal works sung by Emma Albani during her career, 1865-1911. Compiled by Gilles Potvin, 1984©

Bach, J.S.	Mass in B Minor	London, Albert Hall, with Bach Choir, 1911
Beethoven	Missa Solemnis	?
	Mount of Olives	Bristol, 1876
	Mass in C Major	Birmingham, 1876
Benedict, Sir J.	The Legend of St. Cecilia*	Norwich, 1878
Bridge, Sir F.	Callirrhoe*	London ?, 1888
Cherubini	Mass in C Minor	?
Coleridge-Taylor	The Blind Girl of Castél-Cuillé, op. 43 (Longfellow)	Leeds, 1901
Cowen, F.	St. Ursula*	Norwich, 1881
	Ruth*	Worcester, 1887
	The Rose Maiden	Victoria, B.C., 1906
Dvorak	The Spectre's Bride, op. 69*	Birmingham, 1885
	St. Ludmilla, op. 71*	Leeds, 1886
	Stabat Mater, op. 58*	Cambridge, 1891
Elgar	The Apostles, op. 49	Birmingham, 1903
Gounod	La Rédemption*	Birmingham, 1882
	Mors et Vita	Birmingham, 1885
	Gallia	Boston, 1889
	Messe de Requiem	Bristol, 1896
Gray, Alan	A Song of Redemption	Leeds, 1898
Handel	Messiah	Bristol, Birmingham, 1876
Haydn	The Creation	Gloucester, 1877
Hummel	Alma Virgo, op. 89	Albany, 1865
Liszt	The Legend of St. Elizabeth	London, 1886

Macfarren, Sir G.	**Joseph***	Norwich, 1878
	King David*	Leeds, 1883
	St. George's Te Deum	London, 1884
Mancinelli, Luigi	**Isaias***	Norwich, 1887
Massenet	**Marie-Magdeleine**	The Hague, 1888
Mendelssohn	**Hear My Prayer**	Birmingham, 1876
	Elijah, op. 70	Bristol, 1876
	St. Paul, op. 36	?
	Hymn of Praise (Symphony No. 2)	Norwich, 1878
Mackenzie, Sir A.C.	**The Story of Sayid, op. 34***	Leeds, 1886
	The Rose of Sharon, op. 30*	London, 1884
Mozart	**Requiem**	?
Rossini	**Stabat Mater**	?
Stanford, Sir C.V.	**The Voyage of Maeldune, op. 34***	Leeds, 1889
	Te Deum, op. 66*	Leeds, 1898
Sullivan, Sir A.	**The Martyr of Antioch***	Leeds, 1880
	The Golden Legend*	Leeds, 1886
	Exhibition Ode*	London, Albert Hall, 1886

*Sung under the direction of the composer

Lehmann, Liza (1862-1918)	**In a Persian Garden** (cycle of 30 quatrains of Omar Khayam for vocal quartet. Sung with Hilda Wilson, Ben Davies and David Bispham at Monday Popular Concerts.	London, 1896

The Lajeunesse Family Tree

Joseph Lajeunesse
1818 — 30 July 1904

m. Mélinda Mignault
26 May 1827 — 28 March 1856

Marie-Louise-Emma-Cécile Lajeunesse
1 November 1847 — 3 April 1930

    m. Ernest Gye
    ? — 1925

Ernest-Frederick Gye
4 June 1879 — 1955

Marie-Delia (Cornélia) Lajeunesse
31 May 1849 — ?

Joseph-Adélard Lajeunesse
19 August 1850 — 19--

Rose-Délima-Mélina Lajeunesse
26 March 1856 — 1856

Emma at five years of age

Chapter One

A Difficult Childhood

No one could have predicted what lay in store for the little French-Canadian girl from Chambly. A daguerrotype of her at the age of five shows a thin, solemn child staring fixedly at the camera. Her bare, bony shoulders protrude above her print dress, and her dark hair, parted in the middle, is arranged in a style that would be ornate for a modern child but was typical of the period.

She is not a particularly pretty child, as she is too thin and her features are irregular. She appears to be pouting, too, although it may be simply the grim, frozen expression typical of contemporary portraits which took minutes to execute. Or maybe it is something more; there is determination in that little chin and the set expression of the mouth. At five she had already taken the first steps on the path that would ultimately lead to international recognition.

Marie-Louise-Emma-Cécile Lajeunesse was born on 1 November 1847 in Chambly, Quebec. But Emma's autobiography and other sources, give either 1850 or 1852 as the year of her birth. Although her baptismal certificate has yet to be found, the records of the convent where she was educated claim 1847 as the correct year, and dates of Emma's confirmation and First Communion support this choice. Her father, Joseph Lajeunesse was a professional musician, skilled on the violin, harp, piano and organ. Her mother, Mélina Mignault, was the eldest of a family of twelve, and like her husband was very musical. Mélina was sixteen at the time of her marriage to Joseph, who was somewhat older. He had spent five years studying medicine, two more studying sculpture, before choosing a career in music. Appropriately, the couple met while Joseph was organist at St. Joseph's Church in Chambly. They were married at Notre-Dame Church in Montreal on 7 January 1846.

There is no doubt that Joseph was intelligent and musically talented. He also appears to have been ambitious, but somehow his ambitions exceeded his capabilities. Perhaps he drank too much, as one rumor contends, but whatever the cause, he was a wanderer, always seeking better positions. When he settled in Chambly with his bride, it was in an unimposing frame house on the Rue Martel, on property belonging to his father-in-law. It was here that their first child, Emma, was born.

Emma Lajeunesse had a colourful heritage stretching back to the early days of Quebec. The first of her ancestors to emigrate to the Chambly area was Estienne Charles of La Villette, a suburb of Paris. A soldier in the Carignan regiment sent to build Fort Chambly, he arrived there on 30 June 1665. Because Estienne was only sixteen, and probably one of the youngest in the regiment, he was nicknamed La Jeunesse — "the youth". The nickname was ultimately passed on to his descendants as a surname. After two years years at the fort, he married 16-year-old Madeleine Niel, a Parisian girl who had come to Canada as a *fille du roi*. This label: daughter of the king was created to describe the young women sent to New France when there was a need to rapidly increase the population of the colony. These women were given doweries and shipped to the new world where marriages were arranged, often the day the boat docked, to bachelor farmers and fur trappers.

Emma's Canadian roots were well developed on the maternal side, too. The first Mignault was Jean Mignot, of Normandy, who married Louise Cloutier in Quebec in 1648. Their descendant, Pierre-Marie Mignault, was curé of Chambly, and his brother Basile was Emma's grandfather. Rachel McKutcheon, Basile's wife, was daughter of Jean McKutcheon, assistant commissary of Fort Chambly. Jean's father, John, had been a Scottish soldier posted to the fort some time after the battle on the Plains of Abraham.

Until the 1850s, Chambly was a bustling port, site of a modern canal on the Richelieu River. Long a vital waterway flowing south into Lake Champlain, the Richelieu had been the main highway into Iroquois lands. It was partly to protect themselves and their Huron allies from attack by the fierce members of the Iroquois confederacy, as well as to launch attacks against them, that the French built the Fort. The original fort burned in 1702 and was replaced by a stronger structure. Occupied by the French and then the British, it was captured by the rebels during the American Revolution, but later returned to British control. As a result, military strength at the fort was increased during the War of 1812. Although Fort Chambly was an active site in the 1837 rebellion, its importance gradually declined. By 1851 the soldiers were gone, and the new railways were carrying vital river traffic from the canal. While the town undoubtedly felt some of the effects of the worldwide economic depression, farming, the mainstay of much of nineteenth-century Quebec, was still thriving. Wood and grist mills processed the products of farm and forest, and there were wool and cotton mills, too, powered by the Richelieu Rapids. A steamship company, *La Cie de Navigation de Chambly*, linked the town with other communities along the river.

In the year of Emma's birth, Canada was a British colony, or more precisely two, Upper and Lower Canada. The two Canadas comprised a variety of cities, towns and settlements sprinkled among vast stretches of uninhabited land. In the populated areas, political beliefs caused many emotional arguments, and violence was often the outcome of passionately disparate views on language and religion. The memory of the 1837 rebellion was still painful in many minds, kept alive by the efforts of politicians to win compensation for those who had suffered losses in the uprising and the controversy those efforts sparked.

Into this political unrest came the Irish immigrants who reached Canada in 1847. Fleeing the potato famine in their native land, more than 50,000 Irish set out for Canada; less than half survived. Most died of typhus which swept through the coffin-like ships, the quarantine station at Grosse Isle downstream from Quebec City, and the waterfronts of eastern Canadian ports. In Montreal, wealthy citizens began a macabre new pastime, strolling along the quayside to view the dead and dying. But even they were not immune and many died from typhus, including the Mayor of Montreal, John Mills, who contracted the disease while working among its victims.

Luckily, Emma and her family were far enough from Montreal to be safely isolated from most of the rampages of politics and disease. Events outside Quebec probably affected even less these Chambly residents. Before Emma's fourth birthday, Karl Marx had published his *Communist Manifesto*, the gold rush was luring thousands to California, and

A sketch of the house on rue Martel in Chambly where Emma was born. The house, which belonged to Emma's maternal grandfather, has since been destroyed by fire.

the first women's rights convention was held in Seneca Falls, New York. In 1849, Wagner fled to Zurich after the collapse of the Dresden Revolt, proving he was more adept at music than at politics. While, in England, Queen Victoria, supported by her beloved Albert, was already making monarchy synonymous with morality.

Emma had other things than world events to concentrate on. Playing with her toys, and her cousins, her young sister Cornélia (born 1849) and brother Joseph-Adélard (born 1850) kept her occupied. There was work, of course, helping her mother inside the house and out, but there was also time for relaxation, alone or with their largé extended family. In the winter, there was showshoeing, skating, sledding; as the snow melted maple sugar time occupied the thoughts of children and many adults. One of Emma's fondest childhood memories was the taste of the grated maple sugar sprinkled on buttered bread that she had experienced in her grandmother's kitchen. When the weather grew warmer, Emma could play outdoors, boating on the Chambly Basin or the Richelieu with her family, picking flowers in her grandparents' garden, or drowsing in the hot sun. At harvest time, there was a bustle of activity and celebration. And, finally, there was Christmas, the culmination of the French-Canadian year.

It was an important feast, this intertwining of the two main threads of Québécois life: family and religion. Through the frosty hush of a winter's night, families on foot, on horseback, or tucked beneath wool and furs in horse-drawn sleds, converged on the parish church. As the horses stamped and clouded the chill air with their steamy breath, the celebrants entered. Grandparents, middle-aged men and women, newlyweds, adolescents, children and babes-in-arms settled into the hand-hewn pews. The light of the sanctuary lamps and dozens of votive candles cast a warm glow on the carved wooden statues and pictures of saints, the priestly robes and the crèche containing a statue of the Infant Jesus. In dazed wonderment, chilled from the cold walk to the church, then starting to sweat in the crowd, Emma must have absorbed the whole scene. As midnight mass ended, she would have been tired, but too excited to sleep, for after church came *le reveillon*.

Then at the house, as the fragrant, spicy smell of tourtière and other delicacies filled the rooms, the family ate and opened presents. Later the real fun started. A fiddle, traditional musical instrument of Canadian farmers, was likely the first instrument produced, and probably more instruments followed rapidly in Emma's musical family. The rhythms they created set feet tapping and hands clapping, so before long, everyone was dancing or singing. The songs were a mixture of traditional Christmas carols, like *D'où viens-tu, bergère?* and timeless favorites such as *A la claire fontaine*. There must have been a smattering of Scottish songs as well as more contemporary pieces. Maybe, in a poignant moment, someone sang *Un Canadien errant*, the haunting ballad, relatively new, that told of an exiled rebel's love for his Quebec home. But, by this time, the children may have dropped off to sleep, sated with sights and sounds and solid food.

Such celebrations were high points to look forward to in humdrum days of regular routine. For Emma, after the age of four, music was an integral part of that routine.

"I never had a doll," she told a reporter in later years. "The early days of my childhood were so taken up with study that I had little time for play."[1] Emma might have exaggerated somewhat for the sake of publicity, since other memories recounted in her autobiography, *Forty Years of Song*, contradict her claim. Still, it was not an outright lie as much of her childhood was taken up with study. Her mother began her musical education, probably as naturally as other mothers taught their daughters cooking and sewing. Some time in 1852, as she approached her fifth birthday, her father took over her musical training.

At the time, the family was living in Plattsburgh, New York, where they had moved in 1851. Joseph was an organist at the Catholic church, and in their brick house on River Street he also gave music lessons. Years later, Marion Brown, a neighborhood child who was one of his pupils, recalled sitting on a prickly horse hair sofa as she waited for her lessons, envying her playmate Emma for the small black lace caps she wore.

There is no indication of how Joseph treated his paying pupils, but where his own children were concerned he was a hard taskmaster. He insisted on four hours of study each day. Believing in the old adage that haste makes waste, he encouraged Emma to practice slowly, concentrating on every note she sounded. Her fingering at the piano had to be exact, and often she was told to count aloud. Sometimes, she fell asleep at the keyboard.

Joseph's obsession with Emma's training brought criticism from friends. All her life, Emma recalled how one of his closest companions chided him. "Lajeunesse, the strain you place upon the child is too great; believe me, she will be unable to withstand it, and in years to come she will suffer."[2] Emma's father simply laughed.

"And he was right," Emma commented, "though at the time I found such exactitude not a little irksome to my buoyant temperament."[3] On at least one occasion, chafing under her father's rigid discipline, she took advantage of his absence to run outside and play with friends. On his return, Joseph ordered her back to her lessons.

Emma had injured her finger while playing, and although she managed her piano practice despite the pain, the harp was simply too much for her. She stopped playing, sat down beside the instrument and started to read. Eventually, her father investigated and told her to get back to work, but Emma refused and they argued. In a fit of temper, she ran her hand along the strings of the harp. Her injured finger caught on a string, tearing the nail severely. Emma fainted and, as she fell, pulled the harp towards her, so Joseph barely had enough time to stop it from falling on her head. It took Emma a long time to recover from the incident, but her father's insistence on long hours of practice did not change at all.

There are hints that young Emma had much nervous energy. Her thinness, her admission to a "buoyant temperament", her love of drama and histrionics all point in this direction. The love of dramatics came naturally, perhaps, influenced by Aunt Rose-Délima, one of her mother's younger sisters. Aunt Rose told fascinating stories, making up different voices for each character as she went along. She encouraged Emma, Cornélia, their brother and young cousins to act out the tales in costumes they made themselves. It was an ideal, if unorthodox, training ground for Emma's future career.

However, it was her father's more formal instruction which brought the most amazing results. By the age of eight, Emma was playing the harp and piano, and could sight read classical music. She had already appeared publicly, at Montreal's Mechanics' Institute. In her autobiography, she also recalls singing in "the English part of Chambly"[4] and playing various musical instruments, often accompanied by Cornélia.

It would appear the Lajeunesse family did a great deal of travelling between Montreal, Chambly and Plattsburgh.

The idea for Emma to appear on stage did not, apparently, originate with the Lajeunesse family. One day, Emma was practising piano in a Montreal store while her father attended to some business. A Mr. Crawford "a well known Scottish balladist" came in and asked who the musician was. Joseph Lajeunesse explained that it was his daughter, adding, "She can sing a little, too." Immediately Crawford asked if the girl would sing for him. At first reluctant, M. Lajeunesse finally agreed. "I sang not once, but three or four times and the stranger expressed his approval," Emma recalled.[5] When she had finished, Crawford asked if M. Lajeunesse would give permission for Emma to participate in a concert he was organizing with some other local music lovers. It took some persuasion, but M. Lajeunesse finally agreed, and Emma went on to make her first appearance in public. Among the songs she recalls singing was *Robert, Robert, toi que j'aime.*

Most likely the Lajeunesse family saw Emma's public appearances as an opportunity to display her talents, not to mention her father's teaching expertise, without any hint of scandal normally attached to a stage career. After all, she was only a child. There are indications, too, that Emma's singing took second place to other musical talents, in her early appearances.

At any rate, matters of a more serious nature soon required the attention of the Lajeunesse family. On 26 March 1856, another child was born, Rose-Délima-Mélina. This happy event was marred by tragedy. Like so many of her contemporaries, Mélina Mignault Lajeunesse died of childbirth complications. She was only 28, at her youngest daughter's birth, and the baby did not long survive her. In the aftermath of these losses, Joseph Lajeunesse was left to solve the dilemma of how to raise his young children alone.

Chapter Two

Sisters of Sacré-Coeur

Joseph Lajeunesse eventually found the solution to his problem in Montreal. By the mid-1800s, Montreal had already celebrated its bicentennial. A bustling city built on an island, it was one of the ten largest in North America and one of the largest in the British Empire. Shaped vaguely like a huge butterfly resting on the waters of the St. Lawrence River, this island had supported many communities, separated by fields and forests, connected by rough dirt roads. Even Mount Royal itself, for which the city was named, was remote, its slopes owned by several families.

Montreal was a port, and in Emma's childhood the city's focal point was the waterfront. Approaching it from Quebec, a traveller grown weary of forest and tiny farm villages could not help being impressed. The view was magnificent — massive stone wharves jutting into the river against a background of stone buildings. Everywhere were churches: Catholic, Presbyterian, Anglican and others, their spires glittering in the sunshine while boats of every description — barques, river rafts, sleek sailing ships and Indian canoes, crammed the waterfront.

Among its people were Indians from the reservation at Caughnawaga or just returned from fur-trapping in the north often visited Montreal. Habitants in their wooden *sabots*, homespun clothing and colourful sashes, the costumes Cornelius Krieghoff immortalized in his paintings, visited Montreal to sell their produce. There were Yankee travelling salesmen, and their southern cousins, who came here for quite different reasons. Resplendent in their elegant suits and antebellum hooped skirts, the men and women of the southern states visited Montreal to escape the oppressive summer heat of home. Also, there were immigrants, arriving en masse from Ireland or in smaller groups from Scotland, England and other European ports. Among the city's permanent residents were nuns in their simple habits of grey, brown or black with

27

rosaries dangling at their waists, ladies in the latest styles from Paris or London, priests, businessmen and soldiers. For Montreal was a garrison town with British soldiers in the fort on St. Helen's Island.

Montreal had been the capital of Canada from 1844 until Ottawa replaced it in 1857. It boasted fine schools, such as McGill University, and elementary schools as well, for both Protestants and Catholics. With a long tradition of teaching and a religious vocation to carry out their work for the glory of God, nuns and priests were among the best teachers of the time. In smaller schools, the emphasis was naturally on the three R's. Catholic schools added a fourth, religion. Typically, the children of Emma's era would master these basics and return to the family farm, find work in a factory or, if they were lucky, go on to further education. A child from a poor family who showed promise might have his or her education financed, providing he considered a religious vocation. Of course, there were other options for the children of well-to-do families.

Studies at the *collèges classiques* were directed towards professional careers. To have a son who was a doctor, lawyer, poet or priest brought pride to a family, but to have a son in business was quite another matter. French-Canadian men rarely went into the trades or commerce. For women, both French and English, there were few choices. Athough the women's movement had already started with the historic meeting in Seneca Falls, N.Y., it had not affected Quebec traditions. Catholic girls dreamed of only two careers: marriage or a religious vocation; for Protestant girls, there was only once choice. Nevertheless, education had its uses. A well-educated young lady could hope to marry a well-educated man, and so the daughters of privileged Quebecers were given the benefit of a prolonged education in all the essential womanly arts.

Under normal circumstances, such education would probably have not been possible for Emma and Cornélia Lajeunesse. However, their father had obtained a post as music master at a prestigious convent, and his daughters were educated free of charge. Possibly, someone used his influence to help Joseph. The curé of Chambly may have taken an interest in his dead niece's children, and perhaps he may have wanted young Joseph-Adélard to consider training for the priesthood in Chambly. At any rate, Joseph-Adélard eventually became a priest, and certainly did not accompany his father and sisters to Sault-au-Récollet, now part of Montreal.

The convent was a magnificent establishment run by the Sisters of the Sacred Heart (Dames du Sacré-Coeur), a teaching order which came to Canada from France in 1842. Located on Rivière des Prairies, the "back river" of Montreal's northwest shore, the convent was built in 1853. An imposing stone structure with sharp gables, the convent offered pleasant scenery and a comprehensive education.

> This Institution unites to its plan of Education every advantage than can be desired, from a punctual and conscientious care bestowed on the Pupils in every branch of science, suitable to their sex, the most uninterested attention is given to form the manners and principles of the young Ladies, and to train them up to habits of order, neatness and industry,

explained a handbill describing the "Young Ladies' Academy."

> The branches taught are Reading, Writing, Grammar, both English and French, Arithmetic, History, Ancient and Modern, Chronology, Mythology, Polite Literature, a little course of Rhetoric and Logic, Geography, Use of the Globes, Elements of Astronomy, Natural Philosophy, Natural History, Chemistry, Botany, Domestic Economy, Plain and Fancy Needle Work, Embroidery, Marking, Lace Work &c &c &c.
>
> The German, Italian and Spanish languages will be taught if desired, but together with Music, Drawing, Painting &c will form extra charges.

For the regular curriculum, the cost was $100 per year (48 weeks, with four weeks' holiday in summer), plus $10 extra for washing, another $10 for stationery. A year's lessons on the piano cost $30, and harp lessons were $48 for the same period. While no particular uniform was required, the students had to wear special dresses on visiting days: Wednesdays and Sundays. "In summer, the young Ladies dress in Pink Stained Muslin. In Winter, the uniform is Green Merino, rather dark." In addition, each student had to bring her own personal supplies:

> One white dress; eight changes of linens at least; three pairs
> of sheets; two pairs of blankets; a white and black figured
> bobinet veil; a sun bonnet; a knife and a fork; two silver
> spoons; a silver goblet; a work box and a dressing case.

and, to set the minds of Protestant parents at rest, the Ladies
of the Sacred Heart added,

> All the young Ladies in the Institution are required to con-
> form to the Public Worship of the house, but no influence is
> exercised over their religious principles.[1]

How strange and new it must have seemed to Emma! At
least she had the comforting presence of Cornélia and her
father, and, from the very beginning, her musical talents
attracted attention.

As a famous singer, Emma fondly recalled how surprised
the nuns were at her ability to read music. Yet, given her
parents' talents, her father's occupation as a teacher, and the
fact that she was eleven years old when she entered the convent school, there was hardly any cause for their surprise.
What might have amazed them was the calibre of Emma's
talent. Initially, she participated in the music contests organized to encourage excellence in students. But she won so often
that she was finally barred from competition.

Her outstanding talent, her stage appearances, and her
father's position at the school might have turned Emma into
an obnoxious brat. Yet there was a wistfulness about her that
engendered affection. Feeling sympathy for her because of the
long hours of musical practice her father required, as well as
the recent loss of her mother, the nuns often allowed Emma
extra playtime in the convent grounds. In winter, her favourite
pastime was snowshoeing, and because of the longer time she
spent outdoors, she became quite good at the sport.

Another quality which might have helped endear her to
teachers and students was her shyness. Despite her stage
appearances, Emma dreaded public speaking. Father Saché
lectured the students on religion and, from time to time, they
were required to write essays on what they had learned. It was
customary for the author of an outstanding essay to read her
work to her schoolmates, and, on one occasion, Emma's work
was selected. When facing the students and teachers, however,
she found herself in difficulty. "The moment came and I

reached the platform and was going to begin to read, when no sound would come. My voice had fled and I was literally too frightened to speak." Diplomatically, Father Saché reassured her: "Sit down my child; you cannot recite, but I know if you had to sing we should all hear it."[2]

For, although she had been barred from competition, Emma's music contributed much to the school. Every day, rain or shine, summer or winter, the school attended Mass in the convent chapel. On special occasions, Emma sang, her clear soprano lifting the Latin words to the vaulted ceilings, while double rows of worshippers knelt beneath the watchful eyes of sacred statues and pictures.

There were only two ways in which Emma escaped her shyness as a child, through music or through role playing, and the latter had its dangers. At the end of each year, the convent held the *"Jour des Prix"*, where instructors crowned their students for their achievements and awarded prizes. Also, there were speeches and entertainments, including religious tableaux. This was a popular event, where students re-created well known religious pictures.

Emma was intrigued by a picture of St. Anthony being tempted by demons, and remarked that it might be fun to play a demon as one could act devilishly without any fear of punishment. She volunteered for the role, and dressed in black clothes with a painted face and horns, threw herself into the role with great energy. Jumping about, she pinched the poor "saint", made horrible faces, tickled, pulled hair, and carried on so fiercely that she became hysterical, had to be taken away and put to bed.

One of the high points of the decade occurred while Emma was at the convent, for in 1860, the Prince of Wales visited Canada. Eighteen years old, handsome, "about five foot seven, slightly built, has a complexion equal to that of a peach and looks very healthy,"[3] Prince Albert Edward was the object of many a schoolgirl's sentimental daydreams. When he arrived in Montreal in late August to dedicate the newly finished Victoria Bridge and take part in a hectic schedule of celebrations, it was the middle of the summer holidays at Sault-au-Récollet. Yet Emma may have missed a chance to perform for royalty and impress her friends, although she was one of the artists chosen to entertain His Royal Highness.

At what is now the intersection of Peel and St. Catherine streets, a huge, circular structure was raised in a cow pasture. Nearly one hundred metres in diameter, its roof supported by three dozen columns, and lighted by 2000 flickering gas lamps, the pavilion hosted an aristocratic party complete with champagne and caviar one night, and a musical extravaganza the next. This "Grand Music Festival" under the direction of Frederick Herbert Torrington was scheduled to start at seven. But the Prince had not yet returned from an outing, so the concert was delayed an hour. By eight, 6000 people had gathered inside the temporary structure, and the concert began — without the prince. He arrived later, and stayed for only a portion of the programme, which finally concluded about 1 A.M. One of the artists he missed was Adelina Patti, a Spanish-born singer who had already made her New York debut as "the little Florinda". Four years older than Emma, Patti would one day be her colleague and chief rival.

As Emma sang, she could not have known, although she may have dreamed about the possibility, that this would be just the first of her many encounters with royalty. Eventually, decades later and in England she would sing as Albert Edward was crowned King Edward VII.

After the royal tour, Canadians had something quite different to absorb their interests: the American Civil War. Some exiled Confederates even used Montreal as a base for espionage activities. Fortunately, Emma was safely removed from the dangers of war and politics. Her main concerns were her education and her music. Especially her music, for sometime during her years at Sacré-Coeur, she decided to pursue a musical career.

This decision was not made lightly. Those who made their living on stage, whether by acting, singing, reciting or lecturing, were scorned by polite society. Often actresses and female singers were considered little better than prostitutes, thus a stage career was hardly an ideal choice for a young Catholic girl, or any well-bred young girl. Yet, when Emma discussed the matter with Madame Trincano, the convent's Mother Superior, she was encouraged. "God has given you a beautiful voice,"[4] Madame Trincano said, "and I think it is clearly your duty to use it." There could be no harm in pursuing a musical career, at least for a few years, Madame Trincano added. If, after an attempt at a musical career, she felt pulled

32

towards a religious vocation, she could return to the convent. Madame Trincano was an Italian, who wept openly when she heard Emma sing in the convent chapel. One wonders what advice would have been given by a different Mother Superior!

Having received encouragement from this respected advisor, Emma still had a major obstacle to overcome for she needed money to finance her training in Europe. There were no schools in North America which could educate her adequately, and, besides, the connections provided by European teachers and colleagues could prove invaluable. She dreamed of studying at the Conservatory of Paris.

A musical soirée was held at the Mechanics' Hall on St. James Street in Montreal. Assisted by Cornélia, Emma sang and played. Despite glowing advance publicity from newspapers such as *La Minerve*, the evening failed to raise enough money for Emma's education. In her memoirs, she speculated on the reasons. "The French Canadians ... had the old world traditional misgiving of a public career, and especially that dislike for any one belonging to them to go on the stage itself, a feeling which was then very much still alive in Canada, although the idea was already beginning to die out in other countries. Consequently, all help, as they then honestly thought in my best interest, was withheld from me in that quarter."[5]

There was only one thing left to do: move. The Lajeunesse family remembered their days in the United States, and Joseph was convinced that there lay the best possibilities for his daughter's career. There were enough French-Canadians and Catholics in northern New York and Vermont for the family to feel at home, and, with the combined talents of Emma, Cornélia and Joseph, they would be able to raise enough money to send Emma to Europe. On 9 July 1865, she officially left Sacré-Coeur. Shortly afterwards, Emma with her father and sister settled in Albany, New York.

Chapter Three

Albany Years

In the middle of the nineteenth century, Catholics were the predominant religious group in New York state, so Emma found no major change in this area of her life. Since most Catholics lived in cities and urban areas where the best musical opportunities existed, Emma's family choose a city. What better place than Albany, New York's state capital? The city had a population of just under 70,000, so it was both small enough to allow Emma prominence, yet large enough to provide ample opportunities for her talent.

On at least one occasion before moving there from Montreal, Emma had visited Albany, with its imposing granite government buildings. On Thursday, 16 June 1864, Tweddle Hall hosted a "Grand Complimentary Concert to M'lle Emma Lajeunesse, the Famous Young Prima Donna, Vocalist, Instrumentalist, and Composer, only 15 years of age, assisted by her younger sister, M'lle Cornélia Lajeunesse."[1] Among Emma's offerings were "a Grand Fantasia, composed by herself on the well-known song of *When This Cruel War is Over*," a piano duet assisted, undoubtedly, by Cornélia, and a rendering of *The Last Rose of Summer* on the harp.

Emma, her sister and father had given concerts in various other cities between Montreal and Albany, but in the New York capital her career flourished. Shortly after she arrived, she was singing in the choir at St. Joseph's Church, and soon won the position of first soprano. Second only to the Cathedral of the Immaculate Conception in importance, St. Joseph's was a fairly new church at that time. Begun in 1856 when it became obvious that the first cathedral could no longer accommodate its increasingly prosperous and numerous congregation, the new church was completed in 1860. The blue limestone medieval styled structure was one of the handsomest places of worship in the city, boasting a carved woodwork interior, fourteen marble columns, stained glass windows and three marble altars. Another feature parishioners took pride in was the church organ, then the second-largest instrument of its kind in the country. When the original organist quit abruptly, Emma was appointed church organist. She also continued to sing in the choir, as well as direct it. She was well qualified for both positions, for in addition to singing and playing several instruments she also composed and arranged music.

When Emma joined the church choir at St. Joseph's, John J. Conroy was the pastor and Thomas M.A. Burke, the curate. Father Conroy, with his straight, dark hair, bushy brows and determined chin looked more like an Irish boxer than a priest, but his blue eyes twinkled merrily. A friendly man and a favourite with local children, he was also an extremely energetic individual with outstanding foresight. During his time as pastor, he established an orphanage, a boys' school, girls' school, as well as raised money to pay the bulk of the church mortgage. Emma's talent was not unnoticed by his keen eyes, and his influence, first as pastor and later as Bishop of Albany, was invaluable to her career.

Emma lost few chances to exercise her musical talent. Although there were few opportunities for formal training in the entire state of New York, Albany did have several amateur associations, and Emma sang with at least one: the Albany Musical Association. Founded at the Congregational Church on 30 September 1867, it presented Handel's oratorio *Judas Maccabeus* at Tweddle Hall on 28 January 1868. Emma was the chief soloist, and no doubt took part in other oratorios.

As well, there were singing opportunities of a more secular nature. For a while, Emma sang at a hotel in Saratoga Springs, the fashionable spa north of Albany. On 4 February 1868, she had a small part in a concert for Miss Florence E. Rice of Brooklyn. Like Emma, Miss Rice had operatic aspirations, and the money the concert raised would help further her career.

Still, Emma did not always take second billing to another singer. On 25 February of that same year, Cornélia accompanied her at Tweddle Hall. Reserved seats for the concert cost $1.00, all other tickets were 50¢, and Emma had top billing.

Did she ever falter, wondering if the work would ever earn her success? She must have been lonely, at least in the beginning, for she boarded with an Albany family, the Haights, at 100 Grand Street. Fortunately, she seems to have made friends easily, and certainly she had many boyfriends. She had grown into an attractive, slender, dark-haired young woman. Was she tempted to marry and forget her dreams of a career on the stage? She was 18 when she moved to Albany, an age when many of her contemporaries were married. Yet, she confessed to a friend, she was not really interested in the opposite sex — all she wanted was her career.

In her memories, she recalls talking to a friend, probably Annie Haight, about her belief that she had an extraordinary destiny. "I do not know how it is or what it is, but I feel as if I had something in me which will be compelled to come out some day, which I must do, which it will be my duty to do."[2] Madame Trincano's advice and the concept of a vocation, a divinely-inspired calling to a career, had obviously influenced Emma. She was very young when she expressed her feelings to Annie, but her friend looked at her and agreed. "Yes, I think so, too."

Of course, conviction of a great destiny is not enough to make it happen. Emma still had many years of struggle before her. But, thanks to Father Conroy's help, the young "cantatrice" soon got a much-needed boost to her career. In 1868, after a few benefit concerts, the citizens of Albany proudly presented Emma with a purse of money. Joseph Lajeunesse was on hand to see the honour awarded to his daughter. Finally, it seemed, their dreams would be realized for Emma was on her way to Europe.

This photograph (circa 1870) of the young Emma Albani has since been used for the basis of a commemorative Canadian stamp in 1980.

Chapter Four

Singing Lessons in Paris

When Emma sailed for France it was the era of the Atlantic steamer, when the wealthy and aristocratic created a microscopic society in ships' staterooms and saloons. In the enforced proximity of the ocean crossings, which lasted anywhere from ten days to three weeks, the *nouveau riche* rubbed shoulders with the nobility. The high seas were an opportune place to inveigle an introduction to the famous and influential, if one could afford a first class ticket.

In all probability Emma could not for what money she possessed had to be managed carefully, if she were to meet the expenses of her European sojourn. There would be tuition fees and living expenses, and there was no way of predicting how long it would be before she earned any additional funds. In all likelihood, she travelled second class. Resembling the squalor of steerage more than the sumptuousness of first class, the "second cabins" were an afterthought of ship's management. Robert Louis Stevenson was a second class passenger on an Atlantic liner about a decade later, and he reported remarkably few differences between second class and steerage. To be sure, there was crockery on the reserved dining table, but the coffee and tea were indistinguishable, and the food was at best, mediocre. In the cramped, poorly ventilated second-class cabins, one could hear all the sounds of steerage passengers: the moans of the sick, the cries of frightened children, the sobs of men and women who had left behind their homes and families forever.

Fortunately, Emma was spared the heart-wrenching experiences Stevenson reported. Few emigrants left the New World for the Old, and if there were any passengers in steerage, they were the new type of middle class tourists eager to see Europe at economy prices. Once she overcame the double problem of seasickness and nostalgia, she spent much of her time planning her career.

After docking in France and taking a train to Paris' Gare du Nord, Emma made her way to the local Convent of the Sacred Heart. The letter of introduction the nuns of Montreal had given her provided little assistance; for she got a chilly reception at the Paris convent. Possibly the nuns there regarded her as one more provincial whose aspirations surpassed her ability, or perhaps they disapproved of Emma's chosen career. In any event, they did not make her feel welcome, and for a brief moment, alone in the bustling gaiety of Second Empire Paris, Emma must have felt dreadfully vulnerable and afraid.

Not for long, however as she had a second letter of introduction, to a Madame La Baronne de Laffitte. Twice widowed, Madame de Laffitte had been a wife of an operatic tenor and a nobleman. She gladly offered Emma accommodations in her home. To a twenty-one-year-old aspiring singer, Paris was a wonderful adventure. Not only was it an important centre of European music, but also it was the most effervescent, carefree metropolis on the continent (or so it seemed) and one of the most beautiful in the world.

In 1850, Louis-Napoléon, nephew of Napoléon Bonaparte, had seized power. Two years later, he established France's Second Empire, taking the title Napoléon III out of respect for Bonaparte's dead son. Motivated by good intentions, the new emperor set out to revitalize the country and its capital.

So, when Emma reached Paris in the spectacular final days of the empire, she found a city beyond compare. Under the supervision of Baron Haussman, the medieval slums had been cleared — no matter that it left thousands homeless — and replaced with modern new buildings. Lined with trees and lit by gas, broad boulevards were created, and the Bois de Boulogne was opened to offer urban residents the pleasures of the country.

France prospered, expanding its industry and railroads while scientists such as Louis Pasteur worked for the benefit of vintners, industrialists and mankind. As the country flourished, many Frenchmen became rich, and with their newfound prosperity came the urge to spend in new and exciting ways. It was a garish age, when everyone seemed anxious to live life to the fullest. It seemed the best way to do so was ostentation. Fashion was just one area where the desire to impress reached ridiculous levels. The crinoline was very popular, and often skirts were so wide that women had difficulty passing through doorways or sitting in coaches.

Nowhere was the love of display more apparent than at the imperial residences, the Louvre and Les Tuileries. Equerries flaunted their green and gold uniforms as they raced about doing the bidding of the Master of the Horse. The duties of the equerries included caring for the imperial stables for both the horses and carriages housed there were famous. Buckingham, the stallion Napoléon rode at the battle of Magenta, was as well known as the skirmish, which, in typical empire fashion, gave the name to a new colour.

Impressive as the equerries were, they were easily outshone by the Cent-Gardes. Specially selected for their appearance, each man was at least six feet tall. In brilliant blue tunics, white breeches, gleaming breastplates and headpieces topped by horsehair plumes, they were a glorious spectacle. Their effectiveness as bodyguards was secondary to their primary role as symbols of the beauty and might of France.

Unimposing in his own appearance, Napoléon knew how much effect impressive looks could have, and so it was logical for him to choose a beautiful Spanish lady to rule with him. Auburn-haired Eugénie had a scandalous past and was not very intelligent, but she was attractive and dressed well. An Englishman, Charles Frederick Worth, was her favourite designer. As much as the restructured capital, the Cent-Gardes, and her often unfaithful husband, Eugénie symbolized the empty splendor of the French empire.

Initially, at least, the scandalousness of it all must have shocked Emma. Nothing in her convent education or limited stage experience could have prepared her for the gossip of the Imperial court. English visitors, perhaps forgetting the behaviour of their own queen's predecessors, were scandalized at the free-and-easy manners of the court. Few conversational subjects were forbidden, and the name of Napoléon's mistresses, as well as those of other courtiers, were common knowledge. Yet, with the exception of the Princesse Mathilde, cousin and former fiancée of the emperor, no society lady would receive an actress or singer in her home or salon as women who performed in theatres were considered to be of low class.

Still, Emma must have become accustomed to court gossip soon enough. Luckily, she had too many other things to occupy her mind, chief among them her musical education.

Her teacher was Gilbert-Louis Duprez, a retired operatic tenor. Educated at the Paris Conservatory, Duprez had taught singing there until 1853, when he established his own singing academy. One of his most famous students was Marie Miolan-Carvalho, wife of Léon Carvalho, the manager of the Théâtre-Lyrique. Madame Miolan-Carvalho had been the chief soprano there until shortly before Emma's arrival in France, and she continued to draw audiences for several years.

Duprez himself had enjoyed years of popularity, although his debut, in the *Barber of Seville* in 1825, was far from successful. His voice was so weak that critics complained the only place to hear him was in the prompter's box. When 19, Duprez had gone to Italy for further study after this poor beginning. In 1831, he was chosen as an emergency replacement — the role was Arnold in *William Tell*, for which both Duprez and his colleagues knew his voice was inadequate for the part. Moreover, his diminutive size did nothing to enhance his stage presence. One ballet dancer was incredulous at the idea of Duprez as Arnold. "That toad?" she scoffed. "Impossible!"[1]

However, no one had considered Duprez's determination. In his autobiography, *Souvenirs d'un Chanteur*, he wrote, "It required the concentration of every resource of will power and physical strength. 'So be it,' I said to myself, 'it may be the end of me, but somehow I'll do it.' And so I found even the high C which was later to bring me so much success in Paris."[2]

That high C set a precedent for operatic tenors, who were expected to attempt it or admit the superiority of Duprez and other successful competitors. Often, it was a completely unnecessary piece of showmanship, and while many audiences listened anxiously to hear if their favorite would reach the note, most composers shuddered at the corruption of their work.

Still, dedication and showmanship aided Duprez's career. In 1835, Donizetti chose him to create the part of Edgardo in *Lucia di Lammermoor*. Thus he established his career and he was principal tenor of the Paris Opera until 1845.

As he had predicted his efforts cost him dearly. By 1849, Duprez's voice was failing, although he was only 43. Gustave Roger, another tenor, heard Duprez sing and noted in his diary that his voice was "more blemished by passion than time." Yet

Duprez continued to pour himself into his roles, holding his audiences through sheer skill and determination. "That's his own blood, his own life that he is squandering to entice from the public those cries of 'Bravo',"[3] Roger observed. For many, Duprez's reckless effort was the major part of his attraction.

Eventually, the effort was too much. Duprez retired to devote himself full time to the teaching he had begun on a part-time basis in 1842. Such was the man Emma had to teach her, and his example alone provided valuable lessons in what determination could accomplish, and how a voice could be destroyed through over-exertion.

He was an exacting master, insisting that each syllable be pronounced clearly and sung precisely. Nevertheless he recognized talent. Near his school was a small private theatre, where he allowed his more advanced pupils to perform. Here, someone asked about Emma's musical gift. "*Elle a une belle voix et le feu sacré*," he responded. "*Elle est du bois dont on fait les grandes flûtes.*"[4] (She has a beautiful voice and the sacred fire. She is the kind of wood from which great flutes are made.)

Emma had hardly begun her studies when she fell ill: the first symptoms were headache and a slight fever, and then she broke out in reddish spots. The diagnosis: typhoid fever, a malady caused by poor sanitation because at that time Paris still had inadequate drinking water, and the food was often contaminated by unhygienic handling. Typhoid was a killer, and for a time Emma's life was in jeopardy. But Madame de Laffitte was determined the girl would survive to make her operatic debut. Aided by a skilled physician and Emma's youth, she nursed her patient through the illness, until Emma was able to resume her lessons.

While Duprez provided expert advice and instruction, Madame de Laffitte made quite a contribution of her own to Emma's advancement. Emma's benefactor had been married to Jean-Blaise Martin, a tenor of such renown that the parts he had sung and acted were known as "rôles Martin". She told Emma how her husband prepared for a part, and urged her to do the same. First of all, Martin kept social activities to a minimum. If he were to sing at night, he did not speak throughout the day. He kept the house well-ventilated, and dined early so that the digestive process did not disrupt his performance.

Even more important than Madame de Laffitte's advice was her access to important people. One of her relatives was

Madame Carette a *"dame du palais"* at the Imperial court. The Empress had many attendants, chief among whom was the Princesse d'Essling, Grand Mistress of the Household. Then came her lady-in-waiting, the Duchesse de Bassano, and, under her, the *"dames du palais"*. These women witnessed all the important state functions as well as the more intimate, everyday occurrences at the court. Many years later, long after the Second Empire had ended, Madame Carette would evoke romantic memories of the time with her book, *Souvenirs intimes de la Cour des Tuileries.*

Through Madame Carette, Emma was invited to one of the last imperial balls at Les Tuileries. Napoléon and Eugénie hosted many grand functions throughout the year. Between January and Lent, there were four formal balls, each attended by as many as five thousand guests. Under the gilded cupola of the Salle de Maréchaux, the guests danced and exchanged pleasantries with Russians, Hungarians and Persians, all in exotic costumes or flamboyant military uniforms. Just before Lent there was a masked ball, and while there was no dancing during the forty days prior to Easter, there were several concerts. After Easter, the festivities resumed, but with a more casual air. The Empress held *"petits lundis"*, little Mondays, to which she invited the younger members of French society. Normally they were excluded from formal balls at the court, but in the post-Easter season, five or six hundred at a time flocked to Les Tuileries. Emma was invited to one of these evenings.

"I can vividly recall the splendour of the scene and the extreme beauty of the Empress," she wrote.[5] For days before, the women of Paris had speculated on what Eugénie would wear, for the designer Worth had created yet another fabulous costume for her. But news of a death sent the court into mourning. Unwilling to cancel the festivities or to cast a pall over them with a black dress, the Empress dressed in pure white, adding pearls and diamonds as accessories. Emma was completely enchanted with her first glimpse of court life.

Yet she was much more impressed with a non-royal encounter. Madame de Laffitte and her brother knew many artistic people. Musicians and other performers were frequent guests in her home, and thus Emma made valuable associations. One of the people she met was Prince Poniatowski, an amateur musician who had been a pupil of Rossini. Once,

43

Poniatowski arrived with a friend and asked Emma to sing for them. She agreed, singing well enough to earn the praise of both men. Then the prince revealed his companion was Maurice Strakosch, a prominent musician and impresario. "Had I known in advance the reason of their visit, I should probably have been dreadfully nervous, and so most likely to have failed to do myself justice. As it was, I believe I sang quite well, and they told me my voice pleased them greatly, which delighted me so much that I could hardly get any sleep that night for thinking of it."[6]

Prince Poniatowski convinced Emma to travel to Italy for further training. After all, that country was the birthplace of opera. The prince also recommended a teacher, Francesco Lamperti of Milan. Thus on the eve of the Franco-Prussian war, which would see the beautiful new city of Paris beseiged and devastated, and the Second Empire toppled, Emma journeyed to Italy.

Emma Albani in Messina for her debut in April 1870.

Chapter Five

Sicilian Debut

Opera had evolved in Italy, and at the beginning of Emma's career, Italian opera dominated the music world. Although France, England and Germany had operas in the vernacular, Italian was *the* language of the art, just as the English language dominates rock music today. Every sizeable city in Italy had its opera house. La Scala in Milan was an establishment with a heritage stretching back hundreds of years. It provided a fine example for students to emulate, and Emma must have attended some performances there. However, she was not ready to appear on the stage of La Scala. Despite successful performance, she obviously still had much to learn.

Music critic Hermann Klein, who heard Emma sing on numerous occasions, claimed her voice was not a superlative one, certainly not equal to Jenny Lind's or Nellie Melba's. Nevertheless, Klein said, Francesco Lamperti made an excellent singer of her.

Lamperti was a thin man with prominent cheekbones and snow-white sideburns that reached to his collar. He was also a traditionalist who had written several treatises on music, and much more demanding than Duprez. Thus Emma was to have another strict disciplinarian for a teacher. Like Joseph Lajeunesse, Lamperti never passed over a fault as he was a severe critic. He had no time whatsoever for lazy students, yet he worked hard with those who demonstrated dedication and a willingness to learn. Luckily, Emma possessed both qualities. Due to her early training, she could read the most difficult music accurately at first glance. Also she played the piano well, and memorized new parts quickly.

Although North American, Emma overcame some serious disadvantages on her long road to success. There was no operatic tradition in either the United States or Canada, and no conservatory to teach operatic roles. Yet, at the same time, this meant she not tempted to become a member of an unchallenging operatic company in some small city. Lacking a native operatic heritage, she was not bound by chauvinistic prejudices which limited some of her European counterparts. Like most North American singers, she would accept changes easily from Italian to French to German music, without worrying about which was "best". Unlike most of them, she was fluently bilingual in French and English before reaching Europe, and found little difficulty in mastering additional languages.

For Emma's first operatic role, Lamperti chose to train her for *La Sonnambula* by Vincenzo Bellini. The two-act opera about a sleepwalking girl was first produced in 1831 and continued to enjoy immense popularity in the last quarter of the 19th century. However the leading role, Amina, was a difficult one for a novice, for the success of the opera rested almost entirely upon the soprano who sang the part. Lamperti was fully aware of this, and, in fact, had purposely chosen the opera because of the difficulty. "Once you can sing *La Sonnambula* properly," he told Emma, "you can sing any other opera."[1]

After a few months in Milan, she realized she would have to find work as lessons and living expenses had depleted her funds. When one of the operatic managers who routinely visited conservatories and singing schools in search of new talent offered her a position, she eagerly accepted. It would not pay much money because newcomers were seldom well paid, if they were paid at all. Still her living expenses would be covered, and she would not have to finance a "prova" in order to reach an audience. These "provas" or tests were customary in Italy. No sensible manager would pay an unproven singer, and perhaps it was only natural that impresarios exacted fees from hopeful students as insurance against lost income if audiences did not come to hear the new talent. The offer of a season's engagement in Sicily was both a compliment and a welcome chance to improve her finances.

On Lamperti's advice, Emma accepted Messina as the site of her debut, and, also on her teacher's advice, chose *La Sonnambula* as her first opera. Lamperti pointed out that Bellini had been Sicilian, and the audiences in this northeastern island city were certain to be extremely demanding of a performance of their own composer's work. If Emma could impress them, she could be confident of pleasing other audiences with little difficulty.

47

Pleasing an audience was no easy task. Opera was more than a show, it was a social phenomenon. Audiences went to be seen at the theatre as much as to enjoy the music, and it was quite normal for men and women to talk among themselves throughout the performance. Conversation ceased, temporarily, when a favorite soprano or tenor appeared, then resumed again. If a prima donna thrilled an audience, moving them to tears, she might be moved to tears herself by their enthusiastic homage. Applause, cries of "brava! bravissima!" and demands for encores besieged the successful singer. So did bouquets hurled by members of the audience. These floral tributes were a mixed blessing, often evoking tears of pain. Enthusiasts did not always aim carefully, and more than one singer suffered injury after being hit in the face by an airborne bouquet.

Just as passionate as their enthusiasm for a splendid performance was the audience's disapproval of a poor one. Hisses, catcalls, miscellaneous articles thrown at the singer (often with greater accuracy than the bouquets) were accepted expressions of dissatisfaction. And even if a singer performed superbly there was no guarantee he or she would escape unscathed. Audiences could become negative and threatening in seconds. Conductor Arturo Toscanini was once injured for refusing to allow encores at La Scala.

Emma was aware of how changeable an audience could be, and must have been tremendously nervous as she awaited her debut. Her thorough training and limited stage experience brought little comfort. With her first appearance before a critical European audience rapidly approaching, Montreal and Albany must have seemed as distant as the moon.

Still, there was one poignant reminder of home. Shortly before her debut, Signor Delorenzi, Emma's elocution master, suggested a name change as Lajeunesse was too mundane. She must have something more romantic, something which sounded Italian, or European at the very least.

According to Emma's recollection of the event, Delorenzi racked his brain and finally suggested Albani, the name of a nearly-extinct noble family. Emma was flabbergasted. "Did you know I once lived in Albany?"[2] she asked.

He did not, Delorenzi insisted, and Emma took the suggestion as a good omen.

Thus Emma adopted the name, and it was as Emma Albani that she faced the Messina audience in April 1870. They adored her. She had an excellent voice, a well-studied technique, and she was young and attractive. At one point, wrote the opera critic of the *Gazetta di Messina*, the theatre seemed full of madmen. Shouting and clapping, the audience demanded Emma take curtain calls again and again. The new diva appeared, reappeared, then, finally, bewildered by the frenetic enthusiasm of the audience, exhausted by her performance and the tension of preparing for it, she burst into tears.

She was twenty-two, and had developed her voice much beyond her singing in Chambly and the Mechanics' Hall in Montreal. She had much further to travel yet, but, for the time being, she could enjoy the acclaim of Sicilian opera-goers. Their adulation was welcome encouragement, proof to Emma that she did have the talent to reach the top of the operatic world. And, because of her success, and a contract that would pay her £20 a month, she would be able to pay both Lamperti and Delorenzi, as well as save a little money.

Emma spent the entire operatic season in Sicily, chiefly in Messina. Everywhere she appeared, she drew adoring crowds, even the critics were laudatory. On 15 May, the *Sicilian Courier* reported, "The voice of Albani is not made to satisfy listeners ... who 'are all ear' ... but to fill all hearts." And later, writing on her appearance in Acireale, the same newspaper said, "Emma Albani is a privileged creature, in whom both the lady and the artist stand at the same eminence, and in who are in unison the actress and the singer."

She had a natural dramatic flair, cultivated since childhood when she acted out Aunt Rose-Délima's stories, improved upon by acting lessons in Paris, where Sarah Bernhardt's example made performers aware of what heights the art could reach. With such acting added to her fine voice and polished skills, the results were irresistible.

From the distance of more than a century, it is difficult to picture the adulation poured upon the nineteenth century prima donnas. Then, many of best operas were relatively new. Their appeal lasted much longer, because audiences had to wait years to see a certain performance. And, because the performances were live, there was an added element of suspense. So many things could go wrong at an operatic performance: a singer could lose her voice, props might fall apart,

Emma Albani in England, perhaps in the costume for Lucia di Lammermoor

scenery collapse, a fire break out. Because of this, and the relative scarcity of entertainment, live operatic performances were often highly-charged emotional affairs. If an opera were superb, a singer fabulous, excitement could reach fever pitch.

As a result, opera stars had huge followings, becoming objects of intense curiosity. Hardly anything they did went unnoticed. Their pictures were displayed in shops, their clothing and hairstyles noted and frequently imitated. When they appeared in public, crowds of fans gathered to catch a glimpse of their idols. They were showered with gifts and proposals of marriage, and the most favored of all were the "nightingales", the operatic sopranos whose light, almost girlish voices and fabulous costumes seemed to their fans the epitome of Victorian femininity.

In many small theatres, the youngest and most attractive projected their charm cross the footlights, so that audiences were often overwhelmed, entranced. For instance, in her first season in Italy, Emma sang well enough to hold an audience throughout a performance in an open-air theatre despite a sudden shower. While her listeners raised umbrellas, Emma continued to sing from the shelter of the covered stage.

A talented new soprano could draw as much attention as a sensational film star today, and Emma had her share of adulation from the very first. One French traveller recounted how he arrived at an Italian town to find throngs of people gathered in the streets. Suspecting some royal personage was visiting, he asked what was going on. "It's Albani," someone said,[3] as if that simple answer explained everything.

The Sicilians called Emma *figlia di Bellini*, Bellini's daughter, and Emma took it as another good omen that she and the composer shared the same birthdate, 1 November. She certainly was fortunate in her early appearances. When she stayed at Acireale, for instance, she was comfortably lodged in the palace and supplied with food by local residents. Also she received the usual gifts of flowers, jewellry and poetry. One old man, ninety years of age and completely blind, presented her with Mandarin oranges from his own grove every day. Another man, suffering from mental illness, wrapped up all his wife's jewels and priceless lace in shawls and had them delivered to Emma. When she returned them, the man was hospitalized.

51

At the end of her first season, the opera management held a benefit night for Emma. Benefits were routine affairs and all the proceeds of a performance went to one member of the company. Not only was it a great way to add to a singer's bank balance, but also it provided a means of measuring a performer's popularity. A popular singer could be certain of a successful benefit, barring natural disasters and acts of God.

Emma almost was the victim of an unnatural disaster. Just before she was to go on stage on the night of her benefit, someone presented her with a bunch of tuber roses and violets. As the overpowering sweet smell of the flowers gave her a dreadful headache, she had to leave the stage in the middle of the performance. A doctor administered ether, hoping to cure the headache, but Emma passed out. She was unconscious for half an hour. Finally, she was able to return to the stage and complete the performance. The benefit was a success, but, for the rest of her life, Emma loathed tuber roses.

The proceeds from the Sicilian season provided Emma with enough funds to continue her education. She returned to Milan. As news of her success had travelled far, she was offered several engagements. After a brief time with Lamperti, she agreed to perform in Florence, and once again left her teacher for a series of stage appearances.

Emma's reputation preceded her to Florence. Of course, the reports in the various Sicilian newspapers helped, but so did a letter from Francesco Lamperti. Emma's teacher told the Florentine management he was sending them "the most accomplished musician and finished singer" his school had ever produced. All this publicity might have resulted in disaster, raising expectations Emma could not possibly live up to; but the Florentines loved her, just as the Sicilians had.

Flushed with success, Emma visited historic landmarks in Florence, eagerly memorizing all she saw and heard for future reference. In contrast to today's policy of having a professional costume designer, opera singers of the nineteenth century were largely responsible for their own stage outfits. Often they paid little attention to the historic setting of the opera, choosing their costumes out of personal preference or a desire to impress audiences. However, few did attempt to get some hint of historical authenticity, and Emma seems to have been one of these. She visited museums and picture galleries noting period dress, then applying what she saw to her own costumes. When pictures or statues existed of real or fictitious characters who appeared in operas, she searched for and studied them, hoping they would add an inspirational touch to her performances.

For Emma, the high point of this visit to Florence was however, not her own success, nor her trips to the museums, but several encounters with Jenny Lind. The "Swedish Nightingale" was superbly gifted and one of the best known operatic sopranos in the world. During two years of concert tours in the United States, P.T. Barnum had acted as her manager, and Jenny had fond memories of North America. In 1852, in Boston, she married Otto Goldschmidt, her conductor.

Lind was fifty when Emma met her, and had all but retired from the stage. The conversations between the two women could have been awkward, for Jenny was reported to be a cold woman who studiously projected an image of religious piety. Had they talked of their spiritual beliefs there would have been severe disagreements as Jenny was something of a religious bigot. According to one of her friends, in 1871 Jenny pointed out an Italian boy who served muffins, apparently at a hotel or restaurant Lind frequented. "You see that boy?" she asked. "I am trying to conquer myself — to *bear* with him — but — he is a *Roman Catholic!*"[4]

Luckily there was no reason to discuss religion when Emma and Jenny had a common interest in music. Eager to learn all she could, Emma was impressed by Lind's accomplishments, and doubtlessly flattered by the attention the older woman paid her. She tried to memorize all Lind said. But all too soon conversations with her idol and her stay in Florence ended.

Another engagement awaited Emma, for she had been hired for the winter season in Malta before leaving Sicily. At one point, Catanians tried to persuade her to sing in their city instead. They pressed so determinedly, even offering to pay the penalty for breaking her Maltese contract, that the operatic manager from Malta heard of the situation. He made a quick trip to Sicily to reassure himself that Emma would not renege. But he need not have worried, for Emma fully intended to keep her part of the bargain.

Strategically located in the centre of the Mediterranean Sea, Malta was an important military base. The presence of British soldiers and sailors on the island would have a profound effect on Emma's career. Because there was little entertainment on the island, the opera was extremely popular. Emma appeared in various roles, *La Sonnambula*, naturally, *Lucia di Lammermoor*, *Roberto il Diavolo*, and *The Barber of Seville*. She also learned the role of Inez in Meyerbeer's five-act opera *L'Africaine* in two days, after management asked her to replace another singer.

Of all the operas Emma appeared in that winter, *The Barber of Seville* was probably the most popular. First of all, it was the only opera buffa of the five, and so likely to appeal to the many soldiers and sailors who were not regular opera-goers. Secondly, there was the music lesson. In the second act of the opera, Almaviva, the hero, disguises himself as a music teacher in order to meet his beloved Rosina. Although Rossini had written a song for the Lesson Scene, prima donnas traditionally inserted a song of their own selection. Emma began by singing *Carnaval de Venise*, but one night her audience clamoured for *Home, Sweet Home*. Emma sang the wistful ballad, and the audience adored it. From then on, she was encouraged to include it in every performance of the opera. Some nights, the soldiers and sailors shouted for more, and Emma obliged with *The Last Rose of Summer* or *Robin Adair*, or sometimes both. "Perhaps it was fortunate that *Il Barbiere* is a short opera," she wrote years later, "for my 'music lessons' were apt to become longer every night!"[5]

When she was not performing or rehearsing, Emma liked social engagements. She made many friends, including the Governor of Malta Sir Patrick Grant and his wife, the Admiral in charge of the naval base, Sir Cooper Key, and a Colonel McCrea whose influence helped further her career. When the season ended, Emma's benefit concert brought her an unusually high sum of money and scores of gifts. In addition to flowers, poetry and jewels, she received an extra purse of money. At the urging of her many new friends, notably Colonel McCrea, she decided to further her career in London.

In tribute to the young singer, two parallel lines of men-of-war flanked her route out of the Maltese harbour. As her steamer chugged along, Emma must have shed a tear or two in remembrance of all the kindness her new friends had shown her. This was one of the difficulties of a singer's way of life. No sooner did she make the acquaintance of interesting and well-meaning people than she was travelling again to some strange new location. London was still the challenge. Had not everyone insisted she try her fortunes there, assuring her she would succeed as she had in Sicily and Italy and Malta? Despite her growing popularity, Emma must have felt a certain trepidation. Fortunately, she had the buoyant optimism of youth. In later years, she remarked that had she known how important a London engagement was to a singer she would have waited much longer before attempting to find work there.

Before leaving for London, Emma gave one more concert. Whatever her worries, she forgot them, at least temporarily, in Sicily. The mayor of Acireale had asked her to perform at a charity concert for the town's poor, and, remembering the warm welcome she had received there, she could hardly refuse. Afterwards, there were speeches and festive meals, but the round of singing and celebration was brief. Inevitably, Emma boarded another steamer bound for England.

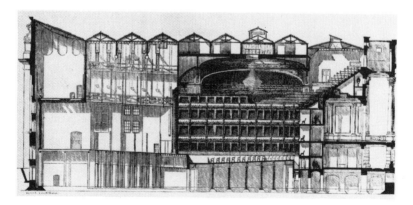

Crowds assembled outside the new Royal Italian Opera, Covent Garden on 15 May 1858. Emma Albani had her debut here fourteen years later.

Chapter Six

Contract at Covent Garden

London was the most populous city in the western world in 1871. When Emma arrived there, London was the capital city of the vast British Empire. Victoria was queen, although she wielded little power, and since the death of Prince Albert in 1861, rarely appeared in public. While the Widow of Windsor, with her plump, round face, would give her name to an era, it was her late husband who contributed much to the Victorian age. Albert was a staunch supporter of progress in almost every form, very much a man for the industrial era.

A century earlier, agriculture dominated the world's economy. Then industrial revolution opened the door to sweeping changes in the way of life of the western world. By 1850, there were over 37,000 kilometres of railway, most of it in the industrialized countries of Europe, such as Belgium, Germany and France with twenty-five percent of the track in Great Britain.

The United Kingdom, was both progressive and prosperous. New industry and invention had brought new wealth to the nation, and the products from around the world which sailed into British ports were purchased eagerly. The wealthy upper classes had always had much leisure time. Now, industrialization further increased income and free time, and with more widespread education which raised their expectations, the middle classes also sought diversion. Consequently, London was able to support not one but two major opera houses.

Under the direction of the bombastic impresario Colonel James Henry Mapleson was Her Majesty's Theatre, called King's Theatre prior to Victoria's accession in 1837. Between 1862 and 1867, Mapleson presented opera at the Haymarket Theatre, but when it burned down moved the opera company to the Drury Lane Theatre, where he remained for a decade.

Mapleson's rival was the Royal Italian Opera at Covent Garden. At one time the garden of a Westminster Abbey convent, the site had been occupied by theatres since December 1732. It offered a wide variety of entertainment, aside from opera. Even Handel conducted there for three seasons between 1735 and 1737. In 1808, the building went up in flames, and a new theatre was erected. In 1847, the Royal Italian Opera company was established here.

This was the second Royal Italian Opera in the city, and the confusing choice of names was deliberate. The first "Royal Italian Opera at Her Majesty's" had been opened in 1793. Disgruntled with the management of Benjamin Lumley, several members of the company at Her Majesty's left to set up a rival troupe at Covent Garden. Among this "Vieille Garde" were Giulia Grisi, then the reigning queen of song in the British capital, Fanny Persiani, Antonio Tamburini and musical director Michael Costa. With director Frederick Beale they ran the opera house from April 1847, but made little money.

The financial situation at Covent Garden improved when Frederick Gye assumed management. F. Gye was the son of a printer, also named Frederick. Gye senior won £30,000 in a state lottery, then went on to various business ventures and a political career. In 1821, he bought Vauxhall Gardens (a resort-type garden on once titled lands) with William Hughes, and, assisted by his son, ran it until 1840.

When Frederick Jr. became manager at Covent Garden, he was in his late thirties, and had considerable experience in theatrical management. If anyone could get the struggling company to survive, Gye was the person.

One of the greatest assets any theatrical manager can possess is diplomacy. It is no easy matter to keep a company of temperamental artists happy. Not only did a nineteenth century impresario have to struggle against fierce professional rivalries, making certain each *primo uomo* or *prima donna* got as many starring roles as his or her chief rival, but he also had to guide the singers toward the roles most suited to their capabilities, and cope with superstition, frayed nerves and fits of pique. It would seem Gye had a flair for handling his volatile company. He always listened to suggestions made by his celebrated singers, and it generally appeared he was carrying out these suggestions. But it was obvious to astute observers that the manager, in fact, acted only on ideas that coincided with his own. If a clash of wills were unavoidable, Gye rarely capitulated, as illustrated by Michael Costa's departure from the company over irreconcilible differences of opinion.

Frederick Gye, manager of Covent Garden

In 1856, the Covent Garden theatre burned again. The paraphernalia of sixty operas, costumes, scenery and props, disappeared in smoke along with the contents of the music and drama library. A few armfuls of papers from Gye's office and a piano were all that were saved, and Gye's personal losses were guessed to be about £30,000.

Everyone assumed Gye's career was over, that he could never recover from the disaster. Gye ignored the pessimists and rented the Lyceum Theatre. In a demonstration of their faith in his managerial abilities, the artists of the Royal Italian Opera company agreed to a cut in salary in order to keep costs down. By October, work had begun on the third and present theatre at Covent Garden. On 15 May 1858, the luxurious new building opened for the first of many operatic seasons.

In 1861, a year after the Prince of Wales visited Canada, Frederick Gye managed a major coup when he lured Adelina Patti away from Col. Henry Mapleson. The beautiful Adelina had promised to sign a contract with the Colonel, but Gye's deal was much more appealing, although only someone as supremely confident as Patti would have agreed to Gye's terms. Adelina would receive nothing for her first three performances at Covent Garden, and if she failed to draw audiences their professional relationship terminated. If Patti succeeded, though, Gye would give her a five year contract. For two performances a week, she would earn £150 a month, and that sum would gradually rise until she was earning £400 during her fifth year with the company.

In June 1871 when Emma arrived in London, she received much the same treatment. There are two different versions of how she signed her first British contract. Emma's Maltese friends had written to both Mapleson and Gye on her behalf. According to Mapleson, Zimelli, the manager of the Maltese theatre, had drawn his attention to this "most charming young soprano, who he assured me was destined to take a very high rank."

Both, a regular subscriber to Mapleson's operas and Colonel McCrea, had also written to the impresario praising Emma. Mapleson, manager of Her Majesty's Theatre, claimed he was quite willing to hear the young woman, and perhaps offer her a contract. In fact, in his memoirs he says Emma's services were "positively promised in a letter written to me by the lady."

On arriving in London, however, Emma directed her cab driver to take her to the Italian Opera. The cab took her to Gye's establishment, and Emma announced her presence by having her card taken in to the impresario. Always searching for new talent, Gye had already heard of the young singer. Mapleson said when Emma was ushered to his rival's presence she assumed that Gye was Mapleson and explained that she had come to sign her contract. "Mr. Gye, knowing that I never made engagements but with artists of merit, gave her at once the agreement she desired." As soon as Gye had the signed contract, he revealed his identity. "He explained there was a manager named Mapleson who rented an establishment somewhere round the corner where operas and other things were from time to time played, but *the* opera, the permanent institution known as such was the one he had the honour of directing."[2] Although he offered to tear up the contract, Emma decided to trust in Gye's self-recommendation and fate.

Mapleson's account of the events can hardly be considered unbiased, and Emma's memories differ somewhat. According to her, Mapleson refused to consider her at all, since he was not in a position to hire new singers at the time. So she went to see Frederick Gye, who had corresponded with her through a Maltese friend. After hearing her sing, Gye offered her a five-year contract.

Emma's excitement at this turn of events was dampened somewhat when Gye explained that he had no immediate openings for her. He also pointed out that, in his opinion, she would be better to make her London debut at the beginning of the next operatic season, rather than during the month remaining in the current one. So, once again, Emma went back to her studies.

Next she went to Como, in Italy. Francesco Lamperti habitually travelled there for the summer months, although it was hardly a vacation, since many of his students followed him to the resort. Despite the burden of lessons, both master and pupils felt revitalized by the majestic panorama of mountains which surrounded them.

With her Covent Garden debut nearly a year away, Emma still needed to manage her finances carefully. She accepted an engagement at the Pergola Theatre in Florence, where she was to sing *Mignon* by Ambroise Thomas. It was

Lamperti's responsibility to coach her in this new role. *Mignon* had premiered in November 1866 at the Opéra-Comique in Paris, so it was a fairly new opera. As a result, neither Emma nor Lamperti had seen it performed. While any accomplished musician could produce an accurate rendition of the words and music, it was the more subtle nuances of the work which perplexed Emma and her teacher. Were they being faithful to Thomas' intentions in their interpretation? And what of Emma's gestures and movements, all the various little pieces of stage props which helped bring an opera to life?

From time to time, serious, emotional arguments erupted between composers and performers over the interpretation of a piece of music. As the creator of the piece, a composer naturally felt he should have the last word on its interpretation. But, as generations of performers argued, it was the singer who brought the work to life. If a prima donna felt a character could be portrayed more vividly by a little embellishment here, a small omission there, surely the composer had no reason to complain.

Emma was aware of the frequent feuds between composers and performers, and was anxious not to get embroiled in one herself. Perhaps this was because of an innate desire to please, a desire reinforced by the demanding natures of her father and successive teachers. Or maybe, having composed music herself, she sympathized with the proprietary feelings of other composers.

She discussed her concerns with Lamperti, and, with his approval, wrote to the Paris music publisher. M. Heugel, asking if he could arrange a meeting with Ambroise Thomas. Heugel agreed, and Emma travelled to Paris, where she had several interviews with Thomas and the stage manager responsible for producing *Mignon* at the Opéra-Comique.

Sixty-year-old Thomas was Director of the Paris Conservatory and an important figure in French music circles, but he patiently reviewed *Mignon* in great detail with the young Canadian, even singing the part to Emma. As they worked, he suggested where she should laugh or sob, or otherwise display emotion in order to bring the young girl stolen by the gypsies more fully to life.

Until the meeting with Thomas, Emma's primary concern had been singing, especially breath control, tone, and voice production. Through her work with the French composer, she realized how important the non-musical portions of the opera, such as the recitatives, were to the overall effect of the work. From that time on, she went out of her way to discuss a work with its composer before her first appearance in it. For instance, if the composer had died, she talked to his close friends and students, or to other musicians who had worked with him.

After two weeks of intensive study with Thomas, Emma travelled to Florence to fulfill her engagement there. In addition to *Le Comte Ory*, she sang *La Sonnambula* and *Lucia di Lammermoor*. It was not until quite late in the winter season that *Mignon* was presented. In spite of the great effort she had put into learning the role, Emma had some misgivings about *Mignon*. It was, after all, a French opera, and had not been accepted well in other Italian towns. But Emma's extraordinary luck and talent helped to make *Mignon* a triumph in Florence. After each performance at the Teatro della Pergola there were several demands for encores, not only of the songs, but also of the recitatives as well.

In retrospect, Emma said *Mignon* marked an important point in her career. Her studies with Thomas and the crowd's enthusiasm for the recitatives taught her the realization that opera was more than music. It was drama, too, and a successful diva was an actress as well as a musician. Emma sang *Mignon* ten times in nine days, doing so well that a telegram was sent to Frederick Gye asking if she could extend her engagement at the Pergola. Gye understandably refused as the London season was about to begin. Once more, Emma was forced to leave the scene of a triumph for a strange new place where her name and talents were almost completely unknown.

Because Covent Garden hired artists on a permanent basis, bringing them back year after year, success there would mean security for Emma. She must have been extremely anxious as she prepared for her London debut. Not only was her professional future at stake, but also she wanted to retain the good opinion of the people she had met in Malta. Many of them were back in England by this time, and Emma had renewed some old acquaintances. Cornélia was there, too, for moral support, so at least Emma had her sister's company as the day of her debut approached. Emma had gone to several performances at Covent Garden when she first visited London in 1871. In her opinion, it was the best opera company in Europe.

It was thrilling to think she could be part of it, but, at the same time, worrisome. Obviously the English audiences were used to the best. Would she be good enough to satisfy them?

Fortunately for Emma, Frederick Gye was an astute businessman who recognized talent. He also realized that excessively complimentary prose only raised expectations to a point where they would be difficult to meet. He kept the announcement of Emma's debut low-key by contemporary standards. The advertisement was brief: "Mlle. Albani, the remarkable young soprano, will appear in an Italian opera at Covent Garden under the management of Mr. Frederick Gye."[3]

Emma's London debut as Amina in *La Sonnambula* occured on 2 April 1872. The critic of the *Musical Times* praised her highly.

> The great event of the month has been the success of Mlle. Albani, who made her début as Amina in 'La Sonnambula.' With a genuine soprano voice, a facile and unexaggerated execution, and a remarkable power of *sostenuto* in the higher part of her register, this young vocalist at once secured the good opinion of her audience, and gradually advanced her position throughout the opera until the final 'Ah non giunge,' her brilliant rendering of which produced a storm of applause which could only be appeased by her appearing three times before the curtain ... there can be no doubt that future performances will fully justify the verdict so unanimously and unmistakably pronounced upon her first appearance.[4]

Other critics were more cautious. One wrote, "The position of the Canadian songstress has yet to be determined; her most ardent admirers rely on her future."[5]

If not a supreme triumph, Emma's debut was a promising start. And, whether she realized it or not, she had reached an important decision time in her life. For the rest of her career she would be associated primarily with the British musical world.

Chapter Seven

A Promising Prima Donna

Emma's successful debut at Covent Garden was a great basis for her career. She had a contract, and for the next few years at least she would not have to worry excessively about money. Moreover, most of her family was back together. Joseph Lajeunesse joined his daughters in London, and apparently acted as Emma's personal manager. His son was studying for the priesthood in Canada. Writing to Heugel, the Parisian music publisher, Emma mentioned studying a new operatic role, adding that her father sent his compliments. Invariably, her letters mentioned her father. One, written in 1873, asked Heugel not to publish a biographical article on her until after her Paris debut, and, above all, not until her father had approved it.

Emma's talent drew enthusiastic response from her London audiences. She had many admirers, and as always was showered with gifts. On her London benefit night, the generosity of her fans nearly proved lethal. As Emma was taking a curtain call, a man in one of the front rows tossed a bouquet and jewel case toward her. In his exuberance the fellow miscalculated the distance and his own strength, thus the case hit Emma in the middle of the forehead. She staggered backwards, and had to be helped to her dressing room by two stagehands. Meanwhile, her now-thoroughly-distraught admirer made apologetic gestures in her direction. Fortunately, the wound was not serious, and the discovery that the case contained a lovely diadem set with brilliants helped in speeding her recovery.

Still, despite such enthusiastic displays of affection there were not enough roles to keep her fully occupied at Covent Garden. Sopranos, and to a slightly lesser extent, tenors, had an extremely possessive attitude toward their roles. Certain operas "belonged" to specific individuals, and no other singer in the company could perform those roles. To do so invited ostracization and the full brunt of a fellow artiste's tempera-

The Royal Box at Covent Garden in 1863 soon after the marriage of the Prince of Wales (later Edward VII) who is seated in the centre to Princess Alexandra of Denmark. Emma Albani sang in the theatre for the royal family, in their castles and at their state affairs.

mental wrath. So, while Emma did sing *Lucia di Lammermoor, Martha*, and *Linda di Chamounix* in her first London season, competition was very lively, thus there were relatively few roles available to her.

Still, there were many other opportunities to exercise her talent while reaching new audiences. Many singers appeared at private concerts in the homes of British aristocracy. A few were sufficiently famous and audacious to demand payment for their performances, but many were content to sing for their supper, knowing the contacts they made could be extremely beneficial to their careers. Emma was one of the latter. She sang at many private homes, including that of the owner of Her Majesty's Theatre, Lord Dudley, who took an interest in the young singer's career. At his house she met the Queen of Holland, "a very amiable and kind hearted old lady"[1] with a long face and fantastically curled coiffure, who complimented Emma on her singing.

It was almost inevitable that Emma encounter royalty, for many were great patrons of the arts, and most had extensive social lives. Almost as a matter of course, Emma was asked to appear at a state concert. These Royal Concerts at Buckingham Palace were exclusive events attended only by members of the royal family, peers of the realm, foreign ambassadors and members of the court. It was a major honour for a singer to be commanded to appear as only the best artists from local theatres were invited. Despite the honour, it was an extremely trying experience for the artists, for the whole affair was heavily bound by tradition and court etiquette. Even the singers' fees were regulated by tradition. Regardless of what she commanded for a regular stage appearance, a singer at a Royal Concert received 25 guineas, no more, no less.

High-strung under normal circumstances, Emma must have been incredibly tense on the night of her first command performance. As her coach neared the palace, she would have seen the Grenadier Guards in full regalia outside. Inside, the cavalry waited, and in the concert room itself were the Yeomen of the Guard in their medieval red costumes and distinctive hats.

The concert room was huge, decorated with frescoes and stained glass windows. Illuminated from the outside, the windows poured vibrant colors into the room. The stage was arranged in the same way as an oratorio stage, tier upon tier of chairs, where performers sat until the concert began.

"Before royalty appears, the singers seat themselves on the stage and remain there until their turn comes to sing. This is always a trial to a singer, who really needs to get into the mood and to warm up to her appearance. To stand up in cold blood and just *sing* is discouraging. The prospect of this dreary deliberateness did not tend to raise our spirits as we sat and waited," recalled American singer Clara Louise Kellogg.[2]

> At last, after we had become utterly depressed and out of spirits, there was a little stir and the great doors at the side of the ballroom were thrown open. First of all entered the Silver-Sticks in Waiting, a dozen or so of them, backing in, two by two. All were, of course, distinguished men of title and position, and they were dressed in costumes in which silver was the dominant note and carried long wands of silver. They were followed by the Gold-Sticks in Waiting — men of even more exalted rank — and finally, by the Royal Party. We all arose and curtesied, remaining standing until their Highnesses were seated.[3]

Queen Victoria rarely appeared at these concerts, leaving the Prince of Wales to take her place. She was not present at Emma's first royal concert.

While the concerts were called informal, knee breeches and silk stockings were *de rigeur* for the men, and as expected the women wore gorgeous dresses and jewels. But the rigid requirements of court etiquette made almost everyone ill at ease, and the pleasure of formal dress was considerably diminished by anxious determination not to commit a breech of etiquette.

The presence of so many dignitaries was enough to upset any performer, especially when the tension of the audience was as palpable as her own. Emma had a particularly difficult time at her first concert. When she finished singing, there was no response — no applause, no bravos, only dead silence. Flustered, she resumed her seat and tried to pinpoint the problems. Was it her singing? Her appearance? Had she committed some unforgivable error? Finally, one of her fellow artists explained it was not considered etiquette to clap during the concert. Those in the know watched the Prince of Wales for if he was pleased, he waved his programme slightly. Enormously relieved, Emma felt her confidence return.

At the end of the performance, the prima donna sang *God Save the Queen*. If there were two leading ladies, they each sang a verse alone, with the other artists joining in for the third. Then the royal party walked past the stage on the way out, murmuring their appreciation and thanks. Once they had gone, everyone relaxed noticeably, and other members of the audience could also express their appreciation. No one, of course, would speak to any artists who had been involved in a scandal. So Adelina Patti, while highly regarded as a singer, was not only denied the satisfaction of applause at royal concerts, but also was icily ignored after her divorce from the Marquis de Caux.

Later, supper was served in another room. There were two tables, one for the royal family and their guests heavily laden with gold plate, and one for the artists. While some singers, like Pauline Lucca, objected to the segregation, most welcomed the free meal and the opportunity to observe closely the most important people in the land.

Among the other celebrities Emma met during her first London season were Sir Julius Benedict and Josiah Pittman. Benedict, who had been knighted a year earlier, was a composer and conductor at Her Majesty's Theatre. With several operas to his credit, he was an important member of the London musical 'scene'. Often, he accompanied Emma on the piano as she sang in private concerts and from him Emma received much professional advice, especially about oratorio. Josiah Pittman, the organist at Covent Garden, also added to Emma's knowledge of this musical form.

Boston conductor B.J. Lang once remarked to operatic baritone David Bispham, "Oratorio is only opera spoiled."[4] Yet the two musical forms had similar roots. In the sixteenth century, Saint Philip Neri taught Bible history by using special hymns and music. At first, oratorios were presented with scenery and costumes, and the performers acted as well as sang their roles. In effect, it was the same as opera, except the themes were always religious. Gradually, though, dramatization fell out of favour with the church, and the theatrical embellishments were eliminated.

Oratorio was performed in the United States, (and Emma had sung them there) but it was in England that the work enjoyed its greatest popularity. Triennial festivals were held in various towns including Birmingham, Leeds and Norwich. There were literally hundreds of performers, many of them amateurs, and rehearsals could go on for a year before the performances. This was serious music, considered by many to be much superior to opera, and many of the most famous musicians, composers and singers of the age were involved with the festivals.

Pittman had worked with many oratorio singers, among them Clara Novello, who was considered the finest of them all. Although Emma never had the opportunity to hear Madame Novello, Pittman gave her much information on the singer's technique. Later in her own career, Emma would be compared to the older singer.

In her autobiography, Emma quoted an article which points out many of the difficulties of oratorio.

> Clara Novello was a great oratorio singer, and a great favourite with the English public. The singing of oratorio is the highest perfection of all, and few are granted the specialised gifts needed to exercise it in perfection. For one really great woman oratorio singer we generally count two or three eminent operatic prima donnas. Oratorio supplies no fictitious aids of scenery, impersonation or story to bring the audience into sympathy with the singer. It is just music in its purest, boldest form, and the artiste who can stand up with 500 stringed instruments behind her and thousands of calm, critical listeners before, and sing "Lift thine eyes" or "O, rest in the Lord" so as to lift every soul there into the Courts of Heaven, must have, as one would think, learned her art among the angels before bringing it down to earth. A voice such as is heard perhaps once or twice in a century, temperament balanced to equal richness and simplicity, these are the conditions necessary for the greatest singers, and for the oratorio singer one more grace is needed — a living faith in the immortal messages to which her voice must lend its wings.[5]

Emma appears to have had both talent and the faith required. Her operatic success and prior experience with sacred music qualified her to sing oratorio, but it was undoubtedly her acquaintance with men, such as Benedict and Pittman which led to her participation in the English festivals. In October 1872, she was hired as a singer for the Norwich Musical Festival.

Madame Thérèse Titiens, one of the most prominent oratorio singers of the day, was a leading artist at Norwich, and Emma was flattered to appear with her on a few occasions. For the young singer, however, the high point of the festival came, innocently enough, out of another singer's misfortune. One of the principal soloists was ill, so the festival committee approached Emma, asking if she could possibly replace the ailing artist. Emma already had a full schedule of her own, with little time to learn or rehearse any new parts. Nevertheless, she promised she would do her best in singing *Angels, ever bright and fair*, as suggested by the committee. A simple card, strategically located, notified the audience of the change in program. Emma was thrilled to see her name presented before thousands of potential listeners in this fashion, and the listeners themselves were not disappointed. As always, Emma Albani managed wonderfully.

It was this willingness to step into a gap left by another singer, to perform not just adequately but superbly, which helped build Emma's reputation in musical circles. She was talented, of course, but so were many other operatic stars and aspirants. She was hard-working, with a solid musical education, qualities which may not have been rare but certainly were not commonplace. At 22, few singers could look back on nearly two decades of intensive musical study.

However, what really set Emma apart from others, was that she was a lady, in the most complimentary sense of the word. The sisters at Sacré-Coeur had taught her manners, given her social graces which enabled her to fit comfortably into the most genteel company. Her own personality, her ingenuous charm, willingness to learn, and total lack of "artistic temperament" made her a delightful co-worker. There were few contemporary artists about whom the same could be said.

Almost as soon as the Norwich Festival ended, Emma was back in Paris for the winter operatic season. The return to the city where she had launched her European studies brought back fond memories, but there was much sadness, too. The Second Empire had crumbled. Napoléon and Eugénie were living in exile in England, and Les Tuileries was a blackened shell. Paris still bore the scars of the Franco-Prussian war, with memories of the bitter siege when starving citizens killed zoo animals for food vivid in many minds. As Emma toured historical sites, museums and picture galleries, she found it impossible to ignore the evidence of the recent conflict.

Still, there was little time for such leisurely pursuits and the recollection they inspired. Emma was unknown to Paris audiences, except, perhaps, by reputation. Once more she experienced the nerve-wracking cycle of rehearsal and anticipation, growing more and more tense as the date of her appearance approached. At least her roles were familiar: *Lucia di Lammermoor, La Sonnambula, Rigoletto*, and this may have lessened her nervousness somewhat. Mostly, she was eager for her appearance to be done as the stress of waiting was worse than any performance could ever be.

She made her debut at the Salle Ventadour or Théâtre-des-Italiens, in the now inevitable role of Amina, in *La Sonnambula*. Although the theatre was small, its acoustics were excellent and more importantly, the audience was impressed. Once again, Emma had proven herself a more-than-competent artist. If there was any doubt of her accomplishment in her mind, it vanished with the arrival of a portrait of her old singing master, signed simply, "Duprez à Albani". Duprez had heard her sing at the Salle Ventadour, and this tribute from one artist to another touched Emma deeply. What better proof that she had truly arrived than to be recognized as an equal by her former teacher?

After Paris, she returned to London for a second season at Covent Garden. This time, she added two new roles to her repertoire, appearing as Ophelia in *Hamlet* and as the Countess in *The Marriage of Figaro*. Again she was warmly received by London audiences. One critic went so far as to say, "Such demonstrations in favour of so young an artiste as were evoked last evening are exceptional in any country."[6]

By this time Emma was being considered as a successor to Adelina Patti, who had dominated the London stage for a dozen years. Adelina was born in Madrid, Spain, on 10 February 1843. Her father, Salvatore Patti, was an opera singer, as was her mother, Caterina Barili. Adelina came close to being born right on stage — her mother sang in *Norma* the night before giving birth.

The family moved to the United States, where Adelina started a theatrical career at a very young age. She was immensely popular with American audiences, so much so, in fact, that when she went to London at the age of 18, the British public regarded the stories of her incredible reputation in the

United States as a gross exaggeration. Her debut at Covent Garden, on 14 May 1861, radically altered that perception. Almost immediately she became a major operatic attraction. Nor was her immense popularity confined to Britain for she made a successful debut in Paris in 1862 and was also a great favorite in Vienna. By the time she married the Marquis de Caux in 1868, she could command tremendous fees. Frederick Gye paid her 200 guineas per performance; a single appearance as Rosina in Frankfurt brought her £400. Eventually, some of her contracts contained clauses entitling her to a percentage of the box-office earnings, and most of them also exempted her from all rehearsals.

Paradoxically, her reputation originated more from her charismatic personality than her musical ability. Her voice was good, but there were better, also she was not an outstanding musician, and her acting ability varied from mediocre to adequate. She was slender, dark-eyed and attractive, but there were more beautiful women on the stage. Moreover, she could be bad-tempered, tyrannical and incredibly unreliable, often cancelling performances at the last minute because of some imaginary ailment, or in a bid for higher fees.

To Adelina, a song was nothing more than a vehicle for her voice. She added, deleted, and altered constantly, driving more than one conductor and composer to distraction. And she made certain her voice would be the sole focus of attention by stepping up to the footlights to deliver her most widely acclaimed arias, regardless of the stage business going on behind her. Much as she wanted the applause of audiences, she never exerted herself, never strained herself.

> Everything divided off carefully according to regime: so much to eat, so far to walk, so long to sleep, just such and such things to do and no others! And, above all, she has allowed herself few emotions. Every singer knows that emotions are what exhaust and injure the voice. She never acted; and she never, never felt![7]

Yet even without any acting, audiences loved Adelina Patti.

There were two reasons. The first was her voice. Few critics were capable of coolly dissecting her performances, for when Adelina sang, everyone was enraptured. Her singing was as effortless and natural as a bird's, and if there were imperfections they only added to the charm. She had the unique ability to move emotions with the most simple song.

Adelina Patti, born in Spain and raised in the United States, led a flamboyant international life as a prima donna.

New York *Evening Post* critic Henry Finck had often pointed out the flaws in Adelina's performances, yet even he would write, "Patti was a nightingale; why ask more of her? In her way, she was absolutely perfect."[8]

This perfection was not in the least diminished by her tempestuous professional and public life. Indeed, her fits of temper, extravagant taste in dress and jewellry, her three marriages, simply made audiences love her more. Patti understood her admirers who considered her vocal talents superhuman. To behave as an average Victorian woman might have destroyed the illusion of semi-divinity her voice created. So, like Olympian gods of legend, she was always doing something outrageous. When the stories of what she had said or done circulated, they simply added another fascinating dimension to the Patti persona.

Yet, there were always newcomers threatening to topple her from her position. Emma Albani was simply one of many, although Adelina may have had some anxious moments after hearing reports about this newcomer from Canada because the critics were saying she would be another Patti. On one occasion, Adelina was walking with her husband along Regent Street and stopped to look at a display of photographs in a shop window. As she stood there, another man glanced at the pictures and remarked to his companion, "There's the portrait of Albani: they say she'll cut Patti out."[9]

Adelina turned on the man, dark eyes flashing. "Thank you sir!" she said icily and walked away.

Emma Albani, possibly dressed for the role of Linda.

Chapter Eight

An Engagement in Russia

Most opera companies realized it was economically unfeasible to remain open throughout the year. Producing an opera was an expensive undertaking, unprofitable if too many tickets remained unsold. If the opera season lasted the entire year, audiences would simply lose interest and managers would lose money. Therefore, in order to protect their investments, managers chose a few months of concentrated production.

Although these short seasons proved beneficial for the management, it made it difficult for a singer (with the possible exception of Adelina Patti, a prima donna) to earn enough for a year's expenses. Certainly the most popular singers earned above-average incomes. By 1875, for example, Emma was being paid £250 monthly for her Covent Garden appearances. But with these high wages went the high expectations of the public, as a successful singer was expected to dress well, eat in fashionable restaurants, patronize fashionable hotels, and entertain lavishly. It was easy to become accustomed to such an elegant lifestyle which was costly to maintain. So, when the opera season ended in one location, artists travelled to others, seeking fresh audiences in cities where no opera companies existed, or displaying their talents to music lovers who knew them by reputation alone.

In the winter of 1873, Emma travelled to Russia. If she had not realized it previously, this journey proved that travel was one of the mixed blessings of an operatic career. American soprano Clara Louise Kellogg had once listed the qualities required of a prima donna. "You must have presence and personality; good teeth and a knowledge of how to dress; grace of manner, dramatic feeling, high intelligence and an aptitude for foreign languages beside a great many other essentials that are too numerous to mention but that you will discover fast enough if you try to go ahead without them!"[1]

One of those essentials was excellent health and stamina, not only for the stage but also for travelling, especially for travelling to Russia. That journey was by train and took several days. Because the operatic season generally started in November, artists accustomed to the milder climates of France, Germany and England were exposed to increasingly cold temperatures as the train travelled northward. The cars were unheated, so veterans of the Russian opera season dressed in fur-lined capes, boots and mittens. There were no dining facilities, so travellers brought along their own food, and often subsisted on crackers. For liquid refreshment, passengers had to carry their own supply or wait until the train stopped, which fortunately, happened frequently. At the numerous stations along the railroad, charcoal fires kept water boiling in huge brass samovars. An attendant added the water to concentrated "essence of tea" and in a few minutes the half-frozen passengers could find comfort in a glass of tea and lemon. Then they returned to the train for more miles of slow creeping across the flat grey Russian landscape.

Dull and colourless as its landscape was in late autumn, Russia was an exotic, almost oriental country in the eyes of most westeners. While Tsar Alexander II had instituted various reforms: freeing the serfs, encouraging self-government in urban areas, and overhauling the judicial system, the country remained in political chaos. Plots and conspiracies abounded while attempted and successful assassinations were commonplace. A great deal of the instigation behind civil unrest came from the privileged classes, so, to divert them, Alexander followed a tradition begun at least in the time of Catherine the Great. He kept his courtiers entertained through sumptuous ceremonies and events at the Imperial court. Opera was one of the most popular of these diversions.

The arrangements for visiting opera companies were unique in Europe, perhaps in the world. In effect, the entire company became a part of the Royal Household during their sojourn in Russia. Lacking native impresarios, a manager was chosen from the best in Europe. It was his responsibility to present the operas, under the watchful eye of the Minister in charge of Imperial Theatres. If all went well, the impresario made a profit, which was his to keep. If the operas lost money, however, the deficit was paid by the Tsar. So great was the Russian people's fondness for music that the Emperor seldom had to pay any of his own funds, but the arrangement must have been a great source of satisfaction to chronically debt-ridden operatic managers.

The Russian experience was a curious one for any operatic company. Describing her visit to St. Petersburg in the 1880s, American singer Lillian Nordica told of the methods the Russians used to protect the artists from the harsh winter climate. Carriages were provided to transport them everywhere, so there was little chance of catching cold during the brief walk between carriage and theatre. The houses where the artists stayed were kept warm by huge porcelain stoves. Double draperies hung from all the windows, with sand to insulate the space between fabric and floor, keeping drafts out.

In short, visiting artists were treated like hothouse plants, rare and precious, much too delicate to be exposed to the cold Russian weather. Yet there was an ominous feeling in the air. Nordica's mother, Amanda Norton, a practical New Englander, wrote to friends from Russia with a warning not to discuss anything in letters "but our legitimate business, which is the music of the opera."[2]

Still, it was easy for pampered visitors to ignore the darker side of Russian life in the dazzle of performances and court events. Emma made nine appearances in Moscow, singing in *La Sonnambula, Rigoletto, Hamlet* and *Lucia di Lammermoor* on what was probably the largest stage in the world. The reaction of Russian music lovers was enthusiastic, if exhausting. Occasionally, Emma had to take twenty or more curtain calls. The audiences were equally lavish in their material displays of admiration. Prince Dolgourky, a relative of the Tsar, sent Emma a bouquet of roses and camelias, surely an expensive tribute in a Russian December. Moreover, tucked amid flowers from opera subscribers was a jewel case containing a fantastic butterfly, "composed of brilliants and rubies, with an enormous emerald forming the body."[3]

After Moscow, the company moved on to St. Petersburg. As soon as the Christmas festivities ended, the second set of performances began, this time with an important difference. The Tsar was often in attendance, and after one performance he appeared on stage to compliment the singers. This was Emma's first encounter with a reigning monarch, and she was "very frightened, but pleased". She found the Tsar both courteous and dignified, and treasured the gifts he gave her. It was customary for the Tsar, who could command performances at any time, to present singers with pieces of jewellry in lieu of payment. Often, the performers returned it to a jeweller for cash, so the same piece might be bought, returned, and presented to another artist several times over. Emma, however, did not part with her imperial gifts, especially treasuring a diamond cross.

In addition to her fellow artists, Emma encountered a familiar face in St. Petersburg that winter. Alfred, Duke of Edinburgh (Affie to his family) was to marry the Tsar's only daughter, Princess Marie, in what would be the most spectacular event of the season. Poor Affie had experienced his share of tribulations in trying to find a bride, and after living in England for several months Emma was undoubtedly aware of at least part of his story.

The Prince's mother, Queen Victoria, was naturally concerned that her children make good marriages. With all the political ramifications involved, though, this was never easy. Alfred had certainly had his share of romances, including one slightly scandalous liaison with a woman on Malta in the early 1860s and another with a commoner. In both instances, marriage was out of the question, for the women were unsuitable as royal wives.

This was not true of Frederika, daughter of the deposed King of Hanover, and a relative of Victoria's. Alfred was quite willing to marry her, and she was a politically suitable choice. But Victoria quashed any hopes of such a match however. Members of Frederika's family had suffered from blindness for three generations, including the deposed King. While Victoria sympathized, she was also concerned for the health of the future royal children and discouraged Alfred's courtship.

She was not any happier with his suit of the Princess Marie, which began in 1869. Victoria despised the Romanovs, considering them arrogant and treacherous. She felt a princess with *"half Oriental* Russian notions"[4] was completely unsuitable for her son. Moreover, the Russian royal family was dissatisfied with the proposed match as well. In 1872, discussions of the marriage stopped. Then, in an ironic about-face, Victoria tried to persuade Affie to renew his courtship of Frederika of Hanover.

The Duke of Edinburgh obviously had other plans for in 1873, negotiations for the Russian marriage were renewed.

Again, Victoria was deeply disturbed with the entire business. In her opinion, the family, especially Prince Alfred, were being humiliated by the Russians interminable discussions and she was still convinced Marie was not the wife for her son. When the engagement was finally formalized later that year, she announced it to the Princess Royal in acid terms. "The murder is out."[5]

Had events proceeded smoothly after the engagement, Victoria might have become reconciled to the idea of the marriage, but the Tsar made matters difficult by refusing to present his daughter to Victoria at Balmoral. The Queen was furious, regarding the pre-nuptial inspection of her future daughters-in-law as an inviolable right. When the Tsarina tried to make peace by suggesting Victoria meet her in Cologne, the English queen became even more indignant. The telegram from the Tsarina suggested they meet in three day's time. "How could I who am not like any little Princess ready to run to the slightest call of the mighty Russians — have been able in 24 hours to be ready to travel! I own every one was shocked." she wrote to her daughter.[6]

In the midst of all this Affie continued with his own plans, and the marriage finally occurred in January 1874. As temporary members of the Tsar's household, the opera company was commanded to provide some of the musical entertainment. For Emma, the royal wedding was the most splendid occasion she had ever witnessed. Outside the Winter Palace, huge furnaces had been constructed for the coachmen to warm themselves as it was a bitterly cold winter. The coachmen would have to wait many hours for their masters, so without the furnaces blazing away many would have frozen to death.

Inside, thousands of white candles burned in the huge reception rooms, their light reflected on the glittering costumes of the guests. Everywhere there were jewels, diadems and necklaces sparkling against velvets and furs and rich embroidery. The women of the court wore "rich robes of cloth of silver or cloth of gold, the bodices of which were shrouded in priceless Valenciennes or Brussels lace, while diaphanous veils floated from their jewelled Russian caps on to the costly trains beneath."[7]

In addition to the State concert, the singers were required to perform during the banquet. Adelina Patti, Sofia Scalchi,

Nicolini, Graziani, and Emma took up positions in the gallery of the White Hall. Below them was the Imperial table, and as the wedding party and guests feasted, the opera stars sang to the accompaniment of conductor Luigi Arditi's music. It was probably the most difficult performance of their careers for this was a wedding with numerous toasts. In royal Russian style, each toast was preceded by a grand flourish of trumpets, regardless of what was going on in the gallery. "Luckily, I escaped this during my song," Emma wrote, "but one or two of the solos were sadly marred by the trumpeters."[8] Amid the cacophony of knives, forks and plates and the conversation of exuberant celebrants, the singers must have felt more than a little frustrated.

After Russia, Emma returned to London for her third operatic season at Covent Garden. In July, she was commanded to perform for the Queen at Windsor Castle. Although Victoria had retired from public life, she still enjoyed music immensely. In fact, it was one of the great personal joys of her life.

By 1874, the year Emma appeared at Windsor, Victoria was 55, a plump little woman with a round face. Contemporary photographs almost always show her with a sullen or petulant expression, but, as one biographer points out, this was caused more by the slow cameras of the day than by an unpleasant personality. Victoria was never a beauty, and what attractiveness she possessed faded quickly under the double burden of monarchy and motherhood. The dourness displayed in photographs and in stories of her chilly regality ("we are not amused") did nothing to enhance her reputation. Yet she had a charming smile which transformed her face; and nothing could evoke that smile as quickly as music. Mendelssohn had been one of her teachers, and, as a teenager, Victoria had adored opera. As well, she loved ballet, folksongs and drama. Anyone who watched the Queen as she listened to her favorite music could not help but notice the marvellous transformation it produced in her face.

At her first command performance for Queen Victoria, Emma sang *Caro nome, Robin Adair*, Gounod's *Ave Maria* and *Home, Sweet Home*. Her royal audience was warmly appreciative. Victoria commented in detail on Emma's voice and singing, making her extensive knowledge of music immediately apparent. Afterwards, she provided Emma with a substantial token of thanks. The Dowager Lady Errol, one of the queen's ladies-in-waiting, was the sister of Mrs. Rich, a friend of Emma's from Malta. When the sisters informed Victoria that the young singer was a Roman Catholic, she had Sir Thomas Biddulph, her Master of the Household, send Emma a pearl cross and necklace. Emma would wear the cross almost constantly for the rest of her life.

Chapter Nine

First American Tour

European artists found a vast market for their highly developed talents on their tours to America. Although cultural institutions flourished in the larger centres of the United States and Canada, they could not compare with similar organizations in Britain, France, Italy or Germany. The very word European meant sophistication and cultural superiority to most nineteenth century North Americans. Europe's long traditions, historical sites, fashionable resorts and royalty created an aura of glamour around any artist who had worked there. As a result, theatrical and operatic managers gradually realized American tours could earn wonderful profits.

In the fall of 1874, Emma appeared in the Liverpool Festival, then sailed for New York and her first American tour. The manager of the tour was Max Strakosch, brother of musician-impresario Maurice Strakosch. Maurice was married to Patti's sister Carlotta, and had conducted American tours in the past. Technically, Emma was still under contract to Frederick Gye, but impresarios often made alternative arrangements, either for their own benefit or that of their artists. So Emma went to the United States with Gye's blessing. Just to make certain no one took unfair advantage of his prima donna, however, Gye sent along his son, Ernest, to be her protector.

This time, Emma travelled first class across the Atlantic. It is unlikely that the operatic company travelled by Cunard lines. While their ships were the safest on the seas, they offered few amenities. Their first-class passengers were not even provided with table napkins, and in one instance when passengers complained, a ship's captain suggested they use their handkerchiefs. Far better to take one's chances in the luxurious accommodation of another line's ships, despite the safety risks which were many, for ships went down with alarming frequency and heavy loss of lives.

Still, voyages were gradually becoming more pleasant. In 1871, the *Oceanic* revolutionized first class travel with quiet midship cabins lighted by oil lamps and heated by steam. The *Oceanic* was also the first ship to have the grand saloon amidships, and boasted separate plush armchairs for diners instead of the customary long benches.

What no one could escape was the motion of the vessel. Emma was a poor sailor, and the Irish Sea was notoriously rough. She invariably spent her first few days of a transatlantic crossing confined to her cabin. Once she got her 'sealegs', though, she generally enjoyed the voyage. Travelling by ship was relaxing, even if the artists spent some time rehearsing or entertaining fellow passengers. By the time the steamer was ready to dock, Emma felt refreshed.

Emma's first North American tour called for appearances in New York and several other cities. Her first appearance using her new operatic surname, Albani, took place on 21 October 1874 at the Academy of Music in New York City. Situated at Irving Place and Fourteenth Streets, the Academy had been New York's principal opera house since 1854. Emma appeared initially in *La Sonnambula*, followed by *Rigoletto, Lucia di Lammermoor* and *Mignon*. Once again, she triumphed. "Mlle. Albani's performance was so striking as to justify the most rapturous applause and so finished as to disarm the coldest connoisseur," reported the *New York Herald*. "Her singing is perfect. It was neither the offspring of wholly French schooling, nor the commonplace teaching of the Italian maestri, but something fresh to the ear, as grateful as the song of the bird."[1]

Emma must have taken enormous satisfaction in her return to the United States and the acceptance of American audiences. But there were some fearful moments during her New York engagement, especially at the beginning of *Lucia* one evening, someone raised an alarm of fire in the theatre. Fortunately, there was no fire, and the audience was so absorbed in the performance that no one panicked.

Fire was a very frightening danger in nineteenth century buildings, and almost every major opera house suffered its consequences at one time or other. The theatres were not only lighted by gas lamps, but also gas lights were used for various stage effects, so it was very easy for a costume or piece of scenery to burst into flames. Conflagration during a performance could turn an audience into a stampeding mob, which might do even more damage than the flames. That such riots were not as frequent as they could have been was often a tribute to quick-witted performers. One tenor put out a fire with the cape of his costume. Another shouted at the audience, shaming them into behaving in an orderly manner, while one conductor placidly led the orchestra as a fire was being fought. Their examples averted tragedy.

Still, even if the theatre were empty, a fire could mean catastrophe with wardrobes, props and scenery burned to ashes. More than one impresario found himself ruined when the flames died down. Few were as fortunate as Colonel Mapleson, whose artists bought fabric and sewed their own costumes in order to fulfill engagements outside London after a theatre fire destroyed the theatre in which they were playing.

In early November, although her schedule would not allow her to visit her birthplace, Emma found time to make a quick trip to Albany. The residents of the New York capital were overwhelmed. "Now she returns, every hand is extended to welcome her back home; from every lip issues heartfelt compliments — in a word, her triumph is of the most genuine nature and character," reported the *Albany Argus*.[2]

Emma gave a concert, singing operatic tunes and popular songs, and met with many friends to talk about the old days and all that had happened since. One related how he had encountered a police-sergeant fresh from hearing Emma sing at the Academy of Music.

The policemen told how he had first heard the prima donna.

She sang for a party of policemen one New Year's Day when we were calling upon the people with whom she lived. The house was on Grand Street, and when we had been there about five minutes, the old gentleman said: "I'm sorry, boys, that I can't offer you anything stiff to drink, but you know my wife is opposed to that sort of thing. Miss Lajeunesse, however, will play for you." Then one of the boys said, "Perhaps Miss Lajeunesse will favour us with a song?" "Why certainly," said she. And I tell you she did sing! She sang some old ballads, simple, old-fashioned songs, but there was more than one pair of eyes that weren't quite dry when she finished, and for a while the boys didn't have much to say. Then I thanked her in the name of the boys, and we got out.

Now she's famous the world over, but I'll bet she never sang better than she did in that little room many years ago for us policemen."[3]

Friends, acquaintances, and strangers poured compliments, good wishes and reminiscences upon Emma. However, they also pried into her personal life. What created the most curiosity was her marital status. After all, she was 27, an old maid by contemporary standards, and there were many rumours circulating through the town about her impending marriage. Finally, the *Albany Morning Express* ended speculation, reporting that "Miss Emma" remained "heart and fancy free."[4] She would remain so for almost four years more, until 6 August 1878 when she married Ernest Gye.

Many prima donnas postponed marriage for the sake of their careers. This was understandable in light of Victorian law which, in effect, allowed a husband to forbid his wife to perform. Husbands were also given control of their wives' earnings, which not only made for difficult situations within a marriage, but also could make life unbearable for managers. Time and time again impresarios found their normally difficult sopranos made completely unmanageable as a result of their husbands' interference. Husbands wanted more money, better publicity, more luxurious accommodations for their wives and for themselves as most husbands travelled with their singing wives. So most managers looked on the husband of a prima donna as a troublemaker. The only thing worse was a husband who was also a singer. If he were mediocre and married to a talented woman, the manager was often forced to include him in performances as a condition of the diva's contract. If they were equally superb artists, a manager had to try to maintain domestic bliss by downplaying professional rivalries, never an easy task. Little wonder that many female singers had contracts containing clauses which prohibited marriage without the permission of the impresario.

In many cases, this seemingly harsh arrangement turned out to be in the best interest of the prima donna as well as the manager. Exposed to all types of people, showered with flowers, poetry, gifts and adulation, young "nightingales" were sometimes vulnerable for what Victorians called cads and bounders. A scandal precipitated by seduction, elopement or an unsuitable marriage could ruin both the prima donna involved and her impresario. According to the morality of the time, a manager was a surrogate father for his unmarried female singers. Women had to be protected, after all, and only a manager of poor moral character would allow a woman under his protection be harmed. Even if he lacked personal integrity, he could not risk the censure of public opinion if some scandal occurred. At the same time, most managers were keenly aware that their "nightingales" attracted impressionable young men whose aristocratic families would be enraged if a marriage took place. Such families wielded enough influence to ruin an impresario, so here, too, a manager had to be constantly careful to stop budding romances.

In his memoirs, Colonel Mapleson recounts one episode involving a singer and romance. Thérèse Titiens noticed an Italian nobleman paying constant attention to contralto Guarducci and brought the matter to Mapleson's attention. The colonel asked what the fellow intended, and when no satisfactory answer was forthcoming, appointed Titiens as duenna to the younger singer. Eventually, the Italian visited Titiens to ask to see his beloved contralto again.

"Yes, as her husband, not otherwise," Titiens replied.[5]

The son of the Duke di Cirilla agreed, but before the wedding could take place permission had to be obtained from his father, the Government of Naples, and the Pope. Mapleson helped speed matters through official channels and arranged for a marriage settlement of £50,000 for Guarducci when the young man succeeded to his father's title. The marriage took place, the couple were married, and a potential fiasco was averted.

Marriages and unsuitable liaisons were only two of the worries which plagued impresarios. Financial troubles were routine; the typical manager was often near bankruptcy several times during the course of his professional career; however, the majority of their problems were caused directly by their artists.

Artists who have struggled out of obscurity or poverty on the strength of talent alone possess enormous quantities of determination. To pursue an artistic career takes courage and a deep conviction that success will eventually come as every outstanding artist encounters discouragement during his or her career, often from friends or family who either directly or indirectly explain the heavy odds against success. Only a particular type of personality can ignore comments of this nature, working constantly towards a career goal against such obstacles. A fortunate few are born rich or find patrons in their youth which greatly aids their careers.

Achieving success underscores an artist's conviction that he or she has been correct. As a performer is often an egoist, to be an outstandingly good performer simply reinforces his or her self confidence. So besides their natural talent the qualities which develop operatic singers into stars — determination, self-esteem, and the ability to ignore the advice of others, are the same which may make them so difficult to handle.

Having struggled long and hard for a position of prominence, no diva was willing to relinquish it to a rival. Arguments frequently ensued if a singer felt another had received preferential treatment. One major area of contention in this regard was the dressing room. Traditionally, the best dressing room was assigned to the prima donna. In many companies, especially those on tour, there might be two or more outstanding sopranos who considered themselves prima donnas. Or the contralto, because of long experience or sheer arrogance, might consider herself the most important female member of the company, thus deserving of the title. In order to prove one's supremacy, it became a serious matter to get the best dressing room.

Mapleson's tour company arrived in Chicago one year to find two dressing rooms in the theatre, one on either side of the proscenium. They were identical in every way, but because Etelka Gerster had used the right-hand room on a previous occasion it was known as the prima donna's room. A performance of *The Marriage of Figaro* was scheduled, with Marie Roze as Susanna and Minnie Hauk as Cherubino. As soon as they arrived at the theatre, the two women began a battle for the right-hand room.

On the day of the performance, Minnie and her maid arrived at three o'clock to deposit her trunks and dresses. An hour later, Marie Roze's maid arrived, and finding the luggage in the prima donna's room, mentioned it to her mistress's husband. He had stagehands remove Minnie's things to the other room.

About 5:30, Minnie's agent came by, switched the contents of the rooms, then installed a padlock on the right-hand room to protect Minnie's costumes. When Marie Roze arrived at six, she hired a locksmith, took possession of the room, and started dressing.

Half an hour later, Minnie arrived, found her rival in the prima donna's room, and flounced off to her hotel in a fit of pique. She absolutely refused to sing until Mapleson's lawyers told she was violating her contract and thus inviting a lawsuit. Finally, halfway through the second act, she appeared, but the "great dressing room disturbance" kept American newspaper readers amused for some time.

There is no evidence Emma ever behaved so wilfully. In fact, when two sopranos were arguing over the disposition of dressing rooms, Emma quietly gave up her own for the sake of peace. Apparently she was so certain of her own talent that a trivial thing like a dressing room was of little consequence.

Chapter Ten

Oratorio and Arthur Sullivan

Almost a decade would pass before Emma returned to America as the intervening years were busy; full of continued triumphs and travel. Following the tour, which took her to Boston, Philadelphia, Baltimore, Washington and Chicago, Emma received an urgent request; would she perform in Venice for the Austrian Emperor and his wife? Emma hurried to Venice as quickly as she could.

Their Austrian Majesties, Franz Josef and Elizabeth, were not quite as prompt. The opera house was full, and *Lucia di Lammermoor*, with Emma in the title role opposite Francesco Tamagno, had begun. Then in the middle of a scene, the orchestra suddenly struck up the Austrian national anthem, for the imperial party had arrived. Once they were comfortably seated, the opera began again.

Such disconcerting interruptions were not unusual; during one performance, in Italy another tenor stopped abruptly in order to sing the national anthem. His patriotic duty done, he lifted his arms in the dramatic gesture he had abandoned moments earlier, then continued as if nothing had happened, much to the chagrin of his leading lady, Nellie Melba. Opera singers may have been the kings and queens of song, but they were definitely subservient to the whims of true royalty.

Emma continued to travel to various locations on the continent in order to appear in operas. She also continued her association with Covent Garden, an association strengthened when she married Ernest Gye, who had just taken over the management of the theatre from his father.

One of four brothers, Ernest would have met Emma soon after she first arrived in London. Their romance likely began during Emma's tour of America in 1874, when Ernest acted as his father's agent. Always excitable, Emma must have been a bundle of nerves in the days preceding the wedding. She and Ernest were married on 6 August 1878 at London's Bavarian Chapel in Warwick Street.

A little shorter than average, with dark hair and a dark beard, Ernest was the envy of many young men for his luck in capturing the affections of the vivacious Mademoiselle Albani. It is unlikely that many of Emma's fans contemplated the problems the husband of a famous prima donna would have to face. Ernest had assisted his father at Covent Garden for several years and undoubtedly possessed some managerial skills. He had, after all, been taught by a master director. Unfortunately, both his father's and his wife's reputations were so great that Ernest was destined to spend his life in their shadows.

Following the wedding, Joseph Lajeunesse returned to Chambly, Quebec, and settled in a large frame house which Emma bought. But, Cornélia stayed in London, and like Ernest, she would spend most of her life in Emma's shadow. While she was a talented pianist in her own right, and for a time taught music to the children of the Spanish royal family, Cornélia Lajeunesse seems to have been content to fill the role of lady-companion to her sister. She never married.

Cornélia's presence must have been a great comfort to Emma. By October, Emma realized she was pregnant. The prevailing attitude towards pregnancy was one of dismay, but whether Emma shared that opinion is difficult to determine, for pregnancy was a "delicate condition" that was never mentioned in polite company. She liked children, certainly, but any joy she felt at impending motherhood must have been tempered with memories of her own mother's difficult pregnancies and death following her fourth childbirth.

Impending parenthood notwithstanding, Emma continued to perform. She appared at the Norwich Festival, singing in *Joseph*, a new oratorio by Professor George Macfarren. Since she was scheduled for another winter season in Russia, as soon as the festival ended she and Ernest slipped away to the continent for a brief vacation.

Newly-married, with a child expected, successful careers and comfortable incomes, Emma and Ernest must have been extremely happy during those first few months. However, their happiness was soon interrupted. Late in November, Frederick Gye was seriously injured in a hunting accident at the lodge of his friend, Lord Dillon, near Oxford. While a friend scaled a wall, Gye held his gun, which accidentally discharged, shooting him in the side. News of the tragedy was cabled to Emma and Ernest, who were about to depart for Russia. They agonized over their course of action, finally deciding to proceed with their engagements. Frederick Gye undoubtedly would have approved, but was never able to say as much to his son and daughter-in-law. He died in early December 1878 after a prolonged struggle that demonstrated both his remarkable constitution and zest for life.

With his death, Emma lost a father-in-law and mentor. Gye had always been solicitous of his stars' well-being, and with her attractive appearance, charming personality and exceptional talent, Emma was a particular pet. He had often cautioned her to preserve her voice, telling her not to sing on consecutive nights. Nor would he allow her to rehearse on the day of a performance for fear of straining her voice. More than anyone else, he was responsible for Emma's popularity in England, indeed almost everywhere, for under Frederick Gye's guidance Emma's career continued to flourish. Understandably, Emma was devastated by the loss, and it was perhaps inevitable that when her son was born on 4 June 1879, he was christened Frederick-Ernest.

There was no question of Emma retiring from public life after the birth of her son, although she did take a few months of rest without performances. She was missed by the public during the fall of 1879. By the next year she was back on stage, and involved in one of the most disastrous incidents of her career.

In January 1880, Emma was scheduled to appear at Milan's La Scala in *Rigoletto* and *Lucia di Lammermoor*. As usual, the Italian audiences were demanding and more than a little hostile, and Emma was not at her best. She had a cold but, unwilling to cancel her engagement, proceeded to sing both roles, relying on her training and experience to carry her through.

Unfortunately, she misjudged her listeners. These were not the adoring British fans who already regarded her as something of a national institution. During a performance of *Lucia*, the audience was offended by a slight, though detectable hoarseness in her voice. They hissed and booed, clamouring so loudly that the performers were scarcely audible. Emma's partner, the tenor Aramburo, after enduring the noise for some time, turned his back on the audience and quietly left the stage, thinking that the boos and hisses were addressed *to him*. Nothing would induce her to complete the engagement at La Scala, and the furious scandal which ensued must have caused her nearly as much misery as the cold and hostile audiences. Fortunately, such fiascos were rare.

Between 1875 and 1883, the year of Emma's return to the United States, she was increasingly involved in oratorio as throughout England it was far more popular than opera. To a large extent, oratorio was a Protestant phenomenon, more common in England and Germany than in the Catholic countries of Europe. Coincidentally, Catholic France and Italy were major producers of opera, at least until the time of Wagner. The ascendancy of oratorio in England and Germany was at least partly due to the fact that they were sung in the vernacular.

Handel, who was known in both countries, had written oratorios which were still popular. During Emma's lifetime, his *Messiah* still drew large audiences, and regular Handel festivals were important events. A great deal of the appeal of oratorio came from the chorus with the power of hundreds of voices. By mid-nineteenth century, however, famous soloists had become an integral part of the presentation.

There were many critics of the practice of assigning solo parts to opera stars. The involvement of professional singers who led vagabond lives, sometimes becoming embroiled in scandal, detracted from the underlying religious nature of oratorio. In 1875, changes were attempted in Worcester. Over protests of the mayor and citizens, Lord Dudley (the same Lord Dudley who owned Her Majesty's Theatre) and the Dean of the Cathedral eliminated soloists and the orchestra. Only choruses and the organ would be used, only anthems and church music sung.

The decision brought about an economic fiasco. The festival towns relied on oratorio to attract the tourist trade, and with no celebrities to draw them, the tourists stayed home or went elsewhere. Worcester shopkeepers hung out black flags, cab drivers decorated their whips with black crepe to show their displeasure, but it was not until 1878 that the town again presented soloists at the festival.

Emma was not directly affected by the changes, for she was singing at Norwich. She rented a house for the week she would be in town, something she did whenever possible. It was "so much quieter than a hotel,"[1] and also enabled her to control her working conditions to some degree, and to allow her son and sister to be with her. She knew how much exertion an operatic career required, for there were many singers whose professional lives had been shortened by poor health. Emma was blessed with an excellent constitution, which she conscientiously maintained. She always tried to master her roles well ahead of schedule, to avoid last-minute panic. Also her healthy routine of enough rest, fresh air and exercise all contributed to a fine performance.

At the same time, Emma managed to enjoy herself thoroughly during her festival engagements. It was not difficult.

> These festivals are, socially, most agreeable functions. They take place in September, one of the months most favoured by the English climate. The principal inhabitants in the town are exceedingly hospitable, and county families fill their houses for the week and bring large parties to the cathedral. Everybody seems to know everybody else, all the cathedral authorities keep open houses, and the town is gay with ladies' light dresses and the flags and decorations with which the townspeople celebrate their festival so long as it lasts.[2]

Among the artists at the Norwich Festival in Emma's first year were Madame Patey and Edward Lloyd. Emma was still not a principal singer, but she did perform in Mendelssohn's *Hymn of Praise* and *St. Cecilia* by her friend Sir Julius Benedict, who was also conducting the orchestra.

The next year, she was a principal soloist at the second Bristol Festival, appearing in *Elijah* and Beethoven's *Mount of Olives* as well as in *Messiah*. She also appeared at the Birmingham Festival that year, under the direction of Sir Michael Costa. Costa was a strict conductor, a musician who demanded perfection from his artists, both in opera and oratorio. He insisted on thorough rehearsals, unlike many of his colleagues, and often became enraged at a performer's careless approach to their work.

One prima donna who wanted to add her own trills and embellishments as well as sing at her own speed when the mood struck, sent Costa £100 in hopes that he would alter his conducting to suit her singing. He returned the money and insisted he would not stay with the opera company if the prima donna remained. She left.

Emma knew Costa's reputation well as he had worked for Frederick Gye and so she approached her first performance with trepidation. Her nervousness, as usual, was unwarranted. After singing *Hear My Prayer*, Costa complimented her, urging her to devote more time to oratorio as she "had the voice and temperament necessary for it."[3]

Indeed, Emma did. Oratorio was definitely not for everyone, although many singers turned to it to help increase their earnings. Some naturally preferred the drama of the opera, and for them oratorio must have been insufferably tedious. Nearly as unbearable was the attitude of the organizers, and, to a lesser extent, the audience. Not only were soloists expected to sing, they were also assumed to have deep religious convictions. Being experienced actors, many operatic singers managed to create a pious image regardless of their personal beliefs. To some degree the image was enhanced by the custom of limiting female soloists to white or black gowns while performing.

Emma had no need to feign piety. She was deeply religious, and since childhood sacred music had moved her profoundly. To the pleasure of the organizers, she was also completely respectable, untouched by any scandal. And, unlike many of her operatic colleagues, she had the necessary talent for oratorio. Without scenery, costumes, and dramatic plots, the shortcomings of other prima donnas were glaringly obvious. As a superbly trained and skillful singer, Emma was wonderfully suited for oratorio. She did not need any pretty embellishments to add to her appealing presentation for an audience.

During the festivals, singers often had the opportunity to sing selections from various operas at concerts. When Emma sang *Casta Diva* from Bellini's *Norma* at Birmingham, she was complimented by Scandinavian composer Niels Gade. "I heard you yesterday, and your singing and voice reminded me of my great compatriot Jenny Lind. Even the veiled quality of the opening andante of the aria was like her — so suited to the prayer."[4] Emma revelled in the compliment, recalling her meeting with the "Swedish Nightingale" years earlier.

Praise came from other sources, too. In 1882, when Gounod's *Redemption* was about to be produced at the Birmingham Festival, Emma had the principal part. Anxious to discuss the composition with Gounod, she travelled to Paris

Charles Gounod and words of appreciation for Emma Albani

and sang the part for him, finishing *From Thy love as a Father* with a very soft high C. Gounod had never indicated how the note was to be sung and confessed to Emma, "I intended that to be forte but I like your way best."[5] That was how she sang it when the work was presented for the first time, with Gounod conducting. He later praised her as "my dear and great interpreter".[6]

The best composers of the day were frequently asked to write music for a specific festival, and in 1880 Emma met one of the most popular in England, Arthur Sullivan. Today, Sullivan is best known for the comic operas which he wrote in collaboration with William Gilbert. While most were great successes during the team's lifetime, making both men wealthy, Sullivan had higher aspirations.

He had always wanted to be a serious musician. As a boy, he was a chorister at the Chapel Royal, and while there won a Mendelssohn Scholarship to the Royal Academy of Music two years consecutively. He was also given a scholarship to study in Leipzig, an important musical centre. As an adult, he conducted and composed, writing such songs as *Onward Christian Soldiers* and *The Lost Chord*. The latter was written in January 1878 after the death of his beloved older brother, Frederic. It immediately became the best-selling song in over forty years. There was even a series of sentiment postcards based on the song, incorporating verses and the scenes they depicted.

Short, handsome despite his plumpness, with black curly hair and dark eyes, Sullivan was a part of the serious musical world. He was a friend of Jenny Lind's and knew Liszt as well as dozens of grand opera singers, musicians, conductors and composers. Because of his own background and his relationships with these people, Sullivan could never be satisfied with his success in light opera. He wanted to create something both profound and enduring. When the opportunity to write oratorios presented itself, Sullivan grasped the challenge. Ironically, his oratorios and other serious work, including *Ivanhoe*, his single grand opera, are rarely performed today.

In 1880, Sullivan's *Martyr of Antioch* was presented at the Leeds Festival, with Emma creating the lead soprano role. The oratorio marked the beginning of a professional relationship between the two which eventually blossomed into friendship. Like many other composers, Sullivan was very careful

Sir Arthur Sullivan who wrote oratorios as well as light opera

about his work. "At rehearsal he never passed over a fault," Emma recalled.[7] He sometimes noted those faults in his diary: in November 1882, for instance he was rehearsing for the Brighton Festival and noted how Zélia Trebelli sang abominably. Emma, who was also rehearsing, received no criticism. In her, Sullivan had found a true professional, someone he could rely on to perform admirably.

So it was understandable that Emma was one of the artists invited to entertain at a dinner celebrating Sullivan's forty-first birthday in May 1883. The Prince of Wales and his brother the Duke of Edinburgh were among the guests. The Duke, an accomplished violinist, was a close friend of Sullivan's, and naturally knew Emma's talent, since she had sung at his wedding. This evening's entertainment turned out to be a novel experience for everyone. After Emma and Paolo Tosti had finished singing around 11:15, Sullivan called the Savoy Theatre on what Victorians called a new-fangled contraption: a telephone. Although the theatre was closed, several performers had gone there at Sullivan's request and sang selections from *Iolanthe* into the telephone for the benefit of his guests. The remote performance must have generated amazement at the wonders of modern science.

Sullivan was more than a considerate host. "He was one of the kindest-hearted men I ever knew," Emma said. Once, Sullivan came to visit when Emma's son, Freddy, was recovering from an illness. The boy was in the nursery having tea, and when he learned this, the bachelor Sullivan exclaimed, "Oh, do let us all go and have a nursery tea."[8] They went upstairs, where the composer presented Freddy with a white toy rabbit. For a long time afterwards, the Gye family referred to dark-haired Sullivan as "The White Rabbit".

Five years after *The Martyr of Antioch* had its debut, Sullivan presented a second oratorio at Leeds, *The Golden Legend*. Like many oratorios, it was based on a poem, the second part of Longfellow's *Christus: A Mystery*. Characteristically, Sullivan had delayed writing the work as long as he could. It was not until the end of June that he rented a country cottage in hopes of eliminating diversions and settled down to work. At first, nothing happened, and Sullivan grew frustrated. "Fearful effort ... awfully tedious and slow,"[9] he wrote in his diary. Finally, the work began to evolve. Working as fast as he could, Sullivan completed *The Golden Legend* on 25

August 1885. There was barely enough time left to rehearse the oratorio before it was presented on 15 October.

Still, Sullivan was satisfied with his work, and as it turned out, the audiences were thrilled. Emma, who set the pattern for singing the role of Elsie, was stunned by the demonstrativeness of the audience. At the première, they stood on chairs, waved programmes and hats, and cheered loudly. Sullivan was nearly moved to tears by the acclamation. *The Golden Legend* was, in Emma's words, "a spontaneous success".

The *Leeds Mercury* described the scene in detail. "Let the reader imagine an audience rising to its multitudinous feet in thundering approval, a chorus either cheering with heart and soul, or raining down flowers upon the lucky composer, and an orchestra coming out of their habitual calm to wax fervid in demonstration. Never was a more heartfelt ovation."[10]

News of the oratorio's success spread. Emma sang excerpts from it to Queen Victoria, who was enthralled by the music. Soon, other members of royalty expressed interest in the work, and attended performances of it when they could. Among those who wanted to hear *The Golden Legend* for themselves were the German royal family, who suggested Sullivan conduct a performance in Berlin. After some discussion, it was agreed that *The Golden Legend* would be performed in March 1886 as part of the German emperor's 90th birthday celebrations. Pattini, a young soprano, would sing the role of Elsie.

The command performance was scheduled for Saturday, 26 March. Sullivan arrived on Tuesday, in the middle of a snowstorm, and tried without success to reach Pattini. Plagued by kidney stones for many years, he was just recovering from another bout of illness and was too exhausted to make his way through exultant crowds to the singer's hotel. So he retired to the comfort of his own hotel room and watched a torch-lit procession wind its way through the darkened streets.

Sullivan wanted the upcoming performance to be perfect. Not only would *The Golden Legend* have to live up to the reports about it, but its composer would be compared with the giants of German music, many of whom had entertained the German emperor during his long life. In the round of socializing which proceeded the performance, Sullivan may have felt twinges of anxiety. They increased when he met Pattini, for he was far from satisfied. "A little *soubrette*, bright little voice, but does not give me the notion of singing Elsie," he noted in his diary.[11]

At the rehearsal on the day of the performance there were still problems. Pattini was "very uncertain in her entries and very shaky in her time". Hoping for the best, Sullivan went shopping for jewellery for the principal artists after the rehearsal. The performance was scheduled for 7:30. By quarter past seven, Sullivan was ready. Pattini was not. It took her ten more minutes, and when she finally did appear, she had forgotten her gloves and had to return to her dressing room for them.

While not a failure, the performance was hardly the "spontaneous success" of Leeds. "It was the most agonising evening I have ever spent," Sullivan told his diary. He was recalled three times before the curtain, but the performance fell far short of everyone's expectations. Embarrassed and upset, Sullivan looked for some way to repair the damage. Knowing that Emma was in Antwerp, he cabled asking if she would recreate her role of Elsie in Berlin. Unable to leave immediately, she promised to come at the end of the week. Then, undoubtedly with the help of the Prince of Wales, who was visiting his German relatives, Sullivan persuaded the court officials to give *The Golden Legend* another chance.

At 7:30 on 2 April, the oratorio was repeated before the German royal family. This time, the performance was more than satisfactory. "Very good performance. Albani superb. Duet encored. Great enthusiasm and ovation at end," Sullivan wrote laconically in his diary.[12] In fact, he was jubilant. In a letter to Hermann Klein, he elaborated on the events of the evening. "It made all the difference in the world. She positively sang her heart out, and, instead of showing the utmost apathy, the Berliners received the work from first to last with enthusiasm."[13] After the performance, Sullivan joined Ernest and Emma for supper. As a token of his heartfelt appreciation, he presented Emma with a diamond bracelet — and a kiss.

In view of their longstanding friendship and mutual admiration of each other's talent, it was appropriate that Emma was a principal soloist at the Leeds Festival in 1898. On the last day of the festival, 8 October, when the chorus cheered Sullivan at the end, he broke into tears and fled from the stage. Afterwards, he went to Emma's rented house for a light supper. When members of the chorus sang to them outside the window, Sullivan invited them in for cigars and champagne. Perhaps he had a premonition that this would be his last time at the Leeds Festival. By the time the next one was held in 1901, Arthur Sullivan had been dead nearly a year.

Chapter Eleven

Home, Sweet Home

By late 1882, Ernest Gye and his brother, Commander Herbert Gye, had reached an uneasy truce with Colonel James Henry Mapleson who had operated a competing opera house in London. The Colonel was never one to forgive and forget[1], but he was sufficiently shrewd to know when a partnership would be advantageous. He accepted a position with the Royal Italian Opera Company as manager of their American tour. In exchange for expenses, a salary of £1000 per year, and control of the troupe, the company received the benefit of the experience Mapleson had garnered during several previous tours of the United States.

Mapleson selected some fine established singers as well as a few newcomers for the group, including Adelina Patti, Minnie Hauk, Fursch-Madi, Dotti, Scalchi, Ravelli, Campanini, Nicolini and Del Puente. Mademoiselle Berghi and Emma were added as Ernest Gye's personal choices.

Most of the company arrived in New York in early October. Almost at once, it was surrounded by controversy. Ernest was being considered for the manager's position with the Metropolitan Opera house, which was still under construction. According to rumours, when the Metropolitan opened the Academy of Music would be closed, thus creating a monopoly of the Italian opera in New York. The newspapers used many lead stories speculating on the eventual outcome of the affair.

Other news soon pushed the controversy aside. Patti arrived and was welcomed by crowds who had waited at the dockside overnight just to catch a glimpse of her. The tour began auspiciously with successful performances in New York. So great was the enthusiasm for opera that impecunious music lovers sometimes pooled their resources to buy a single ticket. They drew lots to see who would enter the theatre first, with the stipulation that no one stay longer than twenty minutes. When time was up, the ticket was passed on to the next member of the group. Anyone who stayed longer than the allotted time would have to reimburse the others for their share of the ticket.

There were plenty of incidents to titillate both members of the troupe and the public during the tour. Just before a matinee on 23 November, Mapleson got word that the tenor, Ravelli, would be unable to perform. He went to Ravelli's hotel room to find the singer in bed. As Mapleson approached, the singer's dog, Niagara, lunged at him. Mapleson ignored the animal, shook Ravelli, who complained that he was tired and his voice was poor. Aided by Madame Ravelli, Mapleson got the singer out of bed, dressed, and over to the piano, where it became apparent there was nothing wrong with his voice. With Mapleson and his wife allied against him, Ravelli turned to Niagara for support. "Est-ce que ton maître doit chanter?" he asked.[1] When the dog growled, Ravelli decided it meant he should forget the performance, flung off his clothes and ran back to bed.

In Philadelphia, another concert was nearly cancelled when rumour spread that Patti was dead, eaten by mice. Actually, she had been bitten on the left ear, as Mapleson explained in his account of how Adelina described the incident to a reporter with the *Philadelphia Press.*

"So you were bitten by rats last evening?" the reporter said.

> "Oh no, it was not so bad as that," replied Patti, laughing heartily as she recalled the adventure. "I hardly, however, like to mention it at all, for I am really so comfortable in this hotel. They do all they can to please me. When I went to bed last evening my maid turned the clothes over for me to get in, when out jumped six mice — a complete family, in fact; nice, fat fellows. I was not frightened; at least, I was only astonished. I took my bon-bon box and scattered some sweetmeats on the carpet so that the tiny intruders should have some supper, and I went to sleep without any apprehension. In the middle of the night, however, something disagreeable occurred, and I was awakened by a sharp pain in my ear. I put my hand to my head when a mouse jumped to the floor, and I felt blood trickling on the side of my cheek. I got up and called my maid, and examination showed a bite on my left ear. It bled a good deal, and to-day my ear is much swollen. I shall not put any bon-bons down tonight," continued Madame Patti, "and when I sleep in the day time I shall place my maid to act as sentry."[2]

Creatures of a different kind caused some serious trouble for Commander Gye, the troupe's treasurer, when he left Philadelphia. His travelling bag, containing money, jewellery, a cheque book and a cheque for $4,400 was stolen. Again, the story was greatly exaggerated. Accounts circulated to the effect that Albani's diamonds had been in the bag as well. Gye spent some time convincing American revenue officials that he had not, as they claimed, smuggled diamonds into the country.

In January, while the group was travelling from city to city, Emma arrived in New York after a rough passage aboard the *Pavonia*. Following a brief appearance there she took a train to Albany. Her return to that city nine years earlier had been heartwarming, but that was insignificant compared to the welcome she now received.

When Emma and Ernest arrived at Albany's Central Depot late on the evening of 15 January 1883, they were met by Professor George Edward Oliver, manager of the music hall. A military band welcomed Emma with various songs, starting with *Home, Sweet Home*. So many people had gathered to greet Emma that it was impossible to move anywhere in the two blocks next to the station.

Emma and Ernest were taken to the Delavan House, and the next morning streams of visitors came to call at the hotel. Ernest, however, had to turn them all away. Tired from her journey, Emma was resting in anticipation of her concert that evening, and to save her voice would speak to no one.

At eight in the evening, Emma appeared at the Music Hall on the corner of South Pearl and Beaver Streets, before a capacity crowd. Amid the plants and flags which decorated the hall she stood out in her pale pink and white silk dress, trimmed with satin, ornamented with flowers on the skirt, diamonds and pearls on the décolleté bodice.

Her contract called for just three songs, for which she would receive $1500, but Emma provided the audience with a wonderful sampling of her far-ranging talents, choosing selections from opera, oratorio and ballads. Afterward, she took four curtain calls, then obliged the audience's longing for more with an additional song, *Home, Sweet Home*. By now everyone, including Emma, was in tears. The concert was a glorious success, and the local newspapers were overwhelming in their praise.

"Mademoiselle Albani has become a matron since she left us fifteen years ago," wrote one, "but there is that sweetness of expression in her pure features and that playfullness about the mouth and eyes which made her beauty of a lasting type and which her friends remember now as the signs of a gentle disposition." Emma expressed her own feelings about her return to the New York state capital. "Although some of my most sorrowful years were passed here, still my recollections of your noble people and warm hearts will be a sweet memory. I would be glad to come often to this city were it possible to do so."[3]

With her various committments, it would never be possible, but Emma made it clear she had not forgotten old friends. Among the gifts she presented was $150 for Father Burke, who had helped so much during the early years of her career. And, to Annie Haight, the girlhood friend with whom she had shared her dreams, she gave a valuable set of pearls. All too soon, it was time to leave in order to fulfill her engagements elsewhere.

From Albany, Emma went to Chicago, where she opened with singing Elvira in *I Puritani*. Despite frigid temperatures, the opera house was full to capacity. The *Inter-Ocean* newspaper reported how Emma won over an initially hostile audience. "The immense audience which was crowded in the hall from parquet to gallery, though cold and critical at first, were warmed up and roused to intense enthusiasm before the second act was completed ... and the triumph of the evening may be justly considered proof positive of Madame Albani's great powers, both as a singer and actress, and not as the tribute of old friends anxious for her success."[4] As Mapleson put it, "Albani was welcomed with an enthusiasm that even Patti might have been proud of."[5]

From Chicago, the troupe travelled to St. Louis, where Albani, Patti and Scalchi all succumbed to colds. It was one of the hazards of winter travelling, often compounded by the difficult conditions the artists had to tolerate. After the final evening performance in St. Louis, the troupe boarded a special train at 1 A.M. When they arrived in Cincinnati, it was ten degrees below zero, and Mapleson had the cars in which the ballet, chorus and orchestra were sleeping shunted into a siding. It may not have been as comfortable as the hotel, but as the principal artists made their way to their accomodations through the cold and snow, many of them must have wished they had stayed with the train.

The group was in Cincinnati to take part in a music festival, which turned into an unparalleled success, even though Henry Abbey tried to create competition by featuring Christine Nilsson at a local theatre. The hotels in the city were so crowded that people slept in corridors, and the music hall had a minimum of 7000 people for each performance. Emma appeared in *Faust* and *The Flying Dutchman* before going to the next city, Detroit.

Then Adelina Patti caught cold again, after she walked through snow to her carriage. She failed to appear as scheduled, disappointing local citizens for the second consecutive year. The cold did not keep her from going out with her husband, Ernest Nicolini, however, and one excursion provided Mapleson with some amusement.

He was staying at the same hotel as Emma and Ernest Gye, and was with them when Emma saw Patti and Nicolini driving by. "Ernest," she said, "They have gone out. We had better leave cards on them at once."[6]

When Patti saw the cards, Mapleson claims, she waited until it was time for Emma and Ernest to go to rehearsal. Then she said to her own husband, "Ernest, they have gone to the theatre. Now is the time for returning their visit."[7]

Ludicrous, perhaps, but such behaviour is easily understood in the light of Victorian social sensibilities. As colleagues, etiquette required the prima donnas call on each other socially from time to time. But Emma and Adelina were professional rivals with different philosophies of life and concepts of morality. The only way to behave in a socially correct fashion and still avoid an awkward confrontation was to call when the other was certain to be absent.

When Adelina's cold grew worse, Mapleson insisted she stay behind while the troupe travelled to Toronto. She was fortunate as something went awry in the train schedule, and the artists were kept waiting from 2 A.M. to 4 A.M. in a bitterly cold station. Then to add to this annoying inconvenience, Canadian customs impounded all their musical instruments, wardrobes and props, claiming they were subject to duty. Only when Mapleson guaranteed the troupe would be out of the country in a few days did the customs officials relent and release the items.

As the only Canadian in the troupe, Emma was welcomed warmly. On the night of 13 February, the second night the company performed, the Grand Opera House on Adelaide Street was filled to capacity. The Lieutenant-governor and other members of Toronto's elite were there, many of them having arrived in open sleighs. Luigi Arditi, the congenial conductor led the national anthem, sparking three hearty cheers from the enthusiastic crowd. More cheers resounded when Emma appeared in the second scene, and it was several minutes before *Lucia di Lammermoor* could proceed.

The first notes of the recitative *Ancor non grimse* proved that the expectations of the audience, however great, were to be fully realized," reported *The Globe*. "It remained, however, for the aria, *Regnava nel silenzio* to demonstrate how just had been the verdict of the European critics as to the rare beauty of her voice. It is a pure, full soprano of great range, and of exquisite sympathetic quality. It has a surprising breath and roundness, and is of unsurpassed eveness throughout all its registers ... given these extraordinary vocal gifts, her appearance completes the charm. A sweet, honest, good face and a fine majestic figure please the eye as much as the voice charms the ears ... Act by act the impression made by her first aria increased until it culminated in the celebrated mad scene in which her perfect control and great resources were fully displayed. [8]

What should have been a complete triumph was marred by the sudden termination of the opera in the final act when Ravelli lost his voice (was his dog, Niagara, growling backstage?). But Emma had completed her role, and the audience was wildly enthusiastic. Their Canadian prima donna was definitely an international talent, and they called her back before the curtains repeatedly, prompting one stage carpenter to remark, "Well, I guess this ain't like a stage play, it's like a political meeting."[9]

Emma had little time to revel in the adultation of her countrymen. The opera troupe had an engagement in Buffalo, which proved so successful that Mapleson was able to charge five dollars per person for standing room on the window sills of the hall. Then the group boarded yet another train, this time for Washington, D.C. There, in addition to public performances, they appeared at a private White House concert before

President Chester Arthur. The artists included Frapoli, Dotti, Fursch-Madi, and Scalchi, but it was Emma who was the outstanding singer completing the program with *Pur dicesti* and *Robin Adair*.

Boston and New York were next, then, by special arrangement, Emma went north to Montreal. On Monday, 26 March, several Montreal city officials journeyed to Rouses Point, New York aboard a private car. At the border, they welcomed Emma and her husband, then made them comfortable for the last leg of the journey.

Back at Bonaventure Station, a large crowd had gathered. The detachment of policemen enlisted to keep order had little success, especially after Emma emerged from the railway car shortly after 9 P.M. So thick was the crowd in their furs and winter woollens that the party had to fight its way to the street.

Outside, in addition to more crowds, they found members of the local snowshoe club had formed an honour guard. In the flickering light of the club's torches, the party settled into four-horse carriages behind a band. As the music played and the crowd cheered, the snowshoers led the way through the streets, the procession moving slowly as Emma waved to Montrealers gathered along the route.

At the Windsor Hotel, so many people had gathered to catch a glimpse of Emma that she could not walk to the hotel and was carried over the heads of the crowd. Once inside, she found many old friends and acquaintances waiting to greet her. It was an exhilarating, exhausting experience, and only a sample of her future receptions.

With only a week to spend in Montreal, Emma found herself rushed in a whirlwind of activities. The day after her arrival, Emma attended a reception at the Hôtel de Ville, Montreal's City Hall. With Ernest on her right and Acting Mayor Rainville on her left, she was escorted to the dais and seated on the mayor's throne.

Alderman Rainville then read a complimentary speech praising Emma as proof that "the most brilliant artistic talent could flower amid the snows of Canada".[10] Written on pink silk, bearing the city arms and names of the reception committee and a circle of hand-painted maple leaves, the scroll was presented to Emma as a keepsake. Then Louis-Honoré Fréchette, a politician and poet known as "le lauréat" read a poem written in her honour, in which he compared Emma to a golden butterfly.

Afterwards, the spectators were presented to Emma. "I remained on the dais, standing for more than two hours, and shaking hands with more than two thousand people, all the kind and notable inhabitants of Montreal who in the goodness of their hearts had come to welcome me." As she and Ernest drove back to the hotel through throngs celebrating the half-holiday declared in her honour, Emma "began to think that after such a commotion and emotion I should never be able to sing another note! It was a most wonderful, stirring, and touching reception, and one which even to the smallest detail I can never forget."[11]

Her first concert was scheduled for that evening, and amid her usual attack of nerves Emma must have found time to reflect on how far she had progressed since singing in the local Mechanics' Hall. How proud her father and family must have been to see her success at Queen's Hall before one of the most warmly receptive audiences she had ever encountered!

The hall was packed, eager to hear their famous singer.

And this enthusiasm was justified simply by the desire to do honour to a lady who began here a musical career that was not to end before she had advanced to the very first place in her royal art ... Had her singing been mediocre, she could have been received with pleasure, but it was not of that class. To most of those present it was a revelation. A voice of exquisite sweetness and wonderful power, compass and freedom, aided by an art so great that it concealed every evidence of itself, filled the room and enthralled those who heard it. Before the last notes had ended a roar of applause rose up from the great audience in every part of the building ... She sang *Ardon gl'incensi* from *Lucia* and *Angels, ever bright and fair*, which showed her great powers in oratorio, and this was greeted as the previous 'effort' if the rippling of a voice as free as the flow of the waters of the pebbly brook can be called an effort, and returning, she sang as an encore *Oh! Luce di quest'anima*. But the crowning item of the evening was when she sang the French song *Souvenirs du jeune âge*![12]

"I wondered what I could sing which would please them all best," Emma wrote, and settled on the song from Hérold's *Pré-aux-Clercs* which she had previously performed at Covent

111

Garden. "It was an inspiration, and made so deep an impression that when I came to the last words, 'Rendez moi ma patrie ou laissez moi mourir,' the whole public rose and cheered me for fully five minutes, and I had to repeat it before I sang *Home, Sweet Home.*"[13] Almost immediately, Hérold's song was republished with Emma's portrait on it and became a great success.

Before the second concert on Thursday, Emma travelled to Chambly and to Sault-au-Récollet to visit the Sisters of Sacré-Coeur. Ernest, Alderman Rainville and his wife accompanied her to the convent, where she was greeted by several former teachers, including Sister Caisso, Sister Ventini, Madame Taillon and Madame Bienvenu. The nuns were charmed by Emma's straightforward simplicity, noting in the journal of the convent that their former pupil had retained "the good principles of her education at Sacré-Coeur"[14] despite the temptations of the worldly artistic life she led.

In the large hall, on the platform where she had found herself too frightened to read her prize-winning essay, Emma spoke to the students who sat under a sign proclaiming "Bienvenue à l'Albani" in huge letters. Later, in the familiar convent chapel, she sang *Ave Maria*. Did she think of Madame Trincano, now dead, and her sympathetic guidance? Or of the hopes and dreams she had cherished as a school girl, now realized far beyond her expectations? Or was the song, as it was meant, simply a heartfelt prayer? When Emma finished, many of her listeners were in tears.

Like the first, her final two concerts were very successful. Together, the three appearances earned $16,000. Before she left, Emma demonstrated her affection for Montreal with a $500 donation to the city's poor and $100 for an "asylum for the blind". Then, filled with the memories of her warm reception in her native land, she returned to New York.

In that American city, Albani made several appearances, including at a concert in which she and Patti performed a duet from Mozart's *Marriage of Figaro*. Despite her success, New York provided a severe disappointment. Although the financiers backing the construction of the Metropolitan Opera had continued negotiations with Ernest, he soon learned that Henry Abbey had been appointed manager. It was a bitter blow for Ernest had provided the architect and backers with detailed information on the structure of Covent Garden as well as its operation. The fact that the organizers had passed him by because he wanted Emma as a leading soloist at the Met, in addition to the organizers' favorite, Christine Nilsson, must have been particularly galling. Ironically, Nilsson did not remain with the company for long.

Mapleson was experiencing difficulty, too, for Abbey had started an active campaign to lure artists away from him to join the Metropolitan. Even Mapleson's daughter-in-law, Madame Cavalazzi, was approached. Patti used Abbey's offer to her as leverage to get a raise in her salary.

The trouble with Abbey and the Metropolitan were the only sour notes in the otherwise triumphant American tour. Although Emma and Ernest's happiness must have been diminished somewhat as a result, they must also have been tremendously satisfied with their second visit to the New World.

Chapter Twelve

Emma and Wagnerian Opera

Emma's career coincided with a time of profound changes in the operatic world. During her lifetime, there was a shift from the Italian domination to an expanded interest in German opera. The composer chiefly responsible for the shift was Richard Wagner.

Born in Leipzig in 1813, Wagner's scandalous private life could provide the basis for an opera. He was expelled from the University of Leipzig, forced to flee from Riga to France in 1839 to avoid debtor's prison, and exiled for his involvement in a revolutionary movement in Saxony a decade later. Unhappily married, he was constantly involved in extra-marital affairs, often with the wives of colleagues and close friends. One of the women, Cosima Von Bülow, daughter of Franz Liszt, was married to a staunch supporter of Wagner, Dr. Hans Von Bülow. Cosima bore Wagner three children before they were finally married. Fortunately, the couple were devoted, and the marriage endured until Wagner's death in 1883.

During these frenetic years, Wagner continued to compose. Through his efforts, opera altered radically. Wagner believed all elements of an operatic work — the plot, acting, scenery, words and music — were equally important. He wanted to eliminate irrelevant components, such as ballet, and to blur the lines dividing recitatives and arias. Although he had not invented the technique, Wagner mastered the use of leitmotiv, melodies or musical phrases which identified themes or characters and helped make the opera into a cohesive whole. Drawing on beloved sagas of Germanic legend, which often had counterparts in other cultures, Wagner created such operas as *Der Fliegende Holländer, Tannhäuser, Lohengrin, Tristan und Isolde, Gotterdämmerung* and *Parsifal.*

Predictably, the sweeping changes Wagner introduced met with hostility in many circles for until the 1870's, opera-going was a largely social phenomenon. In England, people went to the theatre for diversion, and only listened to parts that interested them. During other songs, they talked to friends, played cards, drank and impressed one another with their opulent attire. These activities were encouraged by the practice of leaving all the house lights on during performances, and the behavior of many of the performers who chatted among themselves or played tricks on one another.

In contrast, Wagnerian opera demanded committment from both the audience and performers. Tremendous stamina which ruled out many singers and carefree attendees was required to participate on either side of the footlights. The notion that opera could also be spiritually uplifting, that it might inspire profound thought like a moral tale or oratorio, was also so completely foreign to most opera-goers that they strongly resisted Wagner.

In 1877, a Wagner Festival was held at the Albert Hall in London. Wagner himself attended, since the festival was to raise money for the theatre in Bayreuth, Germany, which performed his works exclusively. According to music critic Hermann Klein, "the adversaries and supporters of Wagnerian art in London were then ranged in three distinct camps. There were (1) those who refused to accept his music under any conditions; (2) those who could accept all he had written down to *Tannhäuser* and *Lohengrin*; and (3) those who worshipped both at the temple and from afar, accepting and rejoicing in everything."[1] Klein goes on to say that the first group was gradually being absorbed by the second. *Tannhäuser* and *Lohengrin* had first been produced more than twenty years earlier. Apparently, it simply took some people longer than others to accept Wagner's work. His latest compositions, such as *Tristan und Isolde* and *Die Walküre*, remained far too revolutionary for most tastes. Few operatic managers would produce the new Wagnerian works for fear of losing money.

As late as the mid-1880s, Wagnerian productions remained high risk propositions in some cities. *Musical New York* reported on one performance of the entire cycle of *Der Ring des Nibelungen*.

The series was given under the special patronage of the Prince of Wales, who loyally remained in his box from the rising to the going down of the curtain, although he confessed afterwards that it was the toughest work he had ever

115

done in his life. When Wotan came on the darkened stage and commenced his little recitative to an accompaniment of discords the Prince took a doze, but was awakened half an hour later by a double forte crash of the orchestra, and, having fallen asleep again, was startled by another climax fifteen minutes afterwards, when he found Wotan still at it, singing against time. At the end of the five weeks Mapleson's share of the losses was $30,000, and the Prince told him confidentially that if Wotan appeared in many more operas he should withdraw his patronage.[2]

Other than the jarring novelty of Wagner's work, another reason many of his operas lost money outside Germany was casting. Without exception, opera companies based their success on the drawing power of their stars, particularly their leading sopranos. The majority of operatic sopranos endeared themselves to their audiences with their light, girlish voices and dainty femininity. As they aged, gained weight and experience, they retained the mannerisms of youth because this is what the audiences expected. The singers were trapped by the stereotypical heroines of French and Italian operas. Amina, Marguerite, Lucia, Gilda were all young girls, innocent and unsophisticated. A fine voice, nice mannerisms, and, if possible, a pretty face and figure were the major requirements for fulfilling these roles. By contrast, Wagner's heroines had more substance. While often young, they were hardly as unsophisticated as the French and Italian heroines, whose lives centred on romance. Certainly love was a major theme in Wagner's opera, but there were deeper undercurrents, too. For most of the prima donnas who starred in Italian operas, Wagnerian roles were completely out of their range. Expecting them to succeed as Isolde or Elsa would be like expecting an actress with no experience but school Christmas plays to triumph as Lady Macbeth. Due to musical snobbery, Italian and French were the languages of opera, and except in their native land, German singers were often considered inferior. Still there were some singers of international calibre whose talent and determination made the transition to Wagner possible. Emma was among them, one of the first and best interpreters of Wagner outside Germany.

Emma's first Wagnerian role was Elsa in *Lohengrin*. As early as 1872 there had been plans to present the opera with Adelina Patti as Elsa, but production was postponed. Patti never did appear in a Wagnerian role, although Henry Finck claimed "she would have given one of her beautiful black eyes to sing and act Elsa, or Elisabeth or Eva."[3] However, Patti eventually did sing excerpts from his works in concert.

One of the difficulties with Wagnerian opera was the German language, as non-Germans found it harsh, guttural and unmelodic, and few opera singers spoke or understood the language. Consequently, the English premiere of *Lohengrin* was an Italian production, with two Frenchmen, Nicolini and Maurel, as Lohengrin and Telramund, two Italians as Ortrud and the King, and an Italian conductor. "It seemed," wrote Hermann Klein, "as though Emma Albani embodies as the heroine the only purely Teutonic realization of the Wagnerian ideal." After a performance of *Lohengrin*, Hans Von Bülow was inspired to embark on a professional musical career. For years he worked closely with Wagner, and if anyone aside from the master could recognize an outstanding Wagnerian performance, it was Von Bülow. He was profoundly impressed with Emma's Elsa when he heard *Lohengrin* at Covent Garden. "If Mlle. Albani ever goes to Germany," he said, "she will show the Germans that Wagner can be sung."[4]

Thus Emma received high praise for her Elsa! In preparation for the Covent Garden premiere, she travelled to Munich to study under Franz Wüllner, conductor of the city's opera house. She already knew the part, having learned it in fifteen days for a performance at New York's Academy of Music the previous year. But she was far from satisfied with her performance. To fulfill her policy of adhering to the composer's intentions, she realized she would have to absorb much more of the technique and atmosphere of German culture and music.

She "went to hear the operas given by the Germans in Germany, so as to acquire a knowledge of all the best methods and traditions known and practised in Wagner's own country. There is nothing which enables an artiste to feel and to understand the actual reality of a rôle so well, both in the music and in the acting, as living so far as possible in its artistic atmosphere while studying it."[5]

As usual, Emma's careful preparation was beneficial. The following year, she introduced *Tannhäuser* to London and subsequently played Senta in *The Flying Dutchman*. In undertaking these roles, Emma distinguished herself from other prima donnas. Wagnerian heroines became something of a specialty, allowing her to demonstrate her talent in new and exciting ways. At the time it was commonly believed singing Wagner was the quickest way to ruin a voice, but Emma's continued success disproved that. The roles offered a chance to grow, both as a singer and as an actress, and Emma not only seized the opportunity but excelled. Moreover, because the Wagnerian roles were something Adelina Patti could never master, the rivalry between the two leading sopranos at Covent Garden was kept to a minimum.

Emma's excellent handling of Wagner's heroines was proven in 1882 when she travelled to Berlin. Obviously she could not sing Italian in the composer's native land, so once again she enlisted Herr Wüllner, this time to teach her the role in German. She appeared with a German cast, including Albert Niemann as Lohengrin. Twenty-one years earlier, Wagner had selected Niemann to create the role of Tannhäuser, and the singer had already performed at Bayreuth. Franz Betz, a member of the Berlin Royal Opera, creator of other Wagnerian roles and himself a Bayreuth veteran, played Telramund. In such outstanding company, any flaws in Emma's performance would be glaringly apparent.

To add to her trial, Kaiser Wilhelm I and other members of the royal family were present and they were not disappointed. "In the German tongue," said the Berlin *Zeitung*, "Albani conjures up the most poetical but likewise the most difficult character of Elsa in *Lohengrin* with such consumate mastery that the auditors are aroused by her to enthusiasm."[6]

After the performance, the Emperor summoned her to the Royal box and bestowed upon her the title *Hofkammersängerin*: royal court singer. It was a rare privilege, shared by a mere handful of artists, most of whom were attached to various royal opera houses. As a further honour, Emma was invited to sing privately for the Empress Augusta.

Ludwig II, the mad king of Bavaria, was one of Wagner's principal patrons, and at one time promised to finance a special theatre for the composer in Munich. On learning how much it would cost to realize Wagner's ambitious plans, Ludwig withdrew his support. But then the city of Bayreuth donated a gift of land for Wagner's theatre and home. With funds raised by Wagner societies around the world, the theatre was begun in March 1872 and opened in August 1876.

118

Although the first cast included some of the finest Wagnerian singers of the period, and the event drew such composers and conductors of the international music scene as Saint-Saëns, Rubinstein and Tschaikowsky, the festival lost money and was closed until 1882.

From the first, the festival was strictly controlled by Wagner. New York music critic Henry Finck, who attended the first festival as a young man, enjoyed the rare privilege of watching rehearsals. Wagner, he said, "attended to every detail of the performance. He would sit near us looking and listening, his face expressing a hundred successive emotions then he would rush onto the stage to show a singer how to pose or phrase. The next moment, he would look down into the orchestra abyss and beg the players 'Not quite so loud, please. Remember that the singers come first.'"[7]

At Bayreuth, everything was carefully controlled in order to produce the desired dramatic effect. Thus artists wore appropriate costumes instead of whatever appealed to them. The orchestra was hidden beneath the stage, with lighting and sets arranged with painstaking care. Those who came to see and hear the operas performed approached as pilgrims approach a shrine. The cumulative effect was a unique, deeply moving experience nearly impossible to duplicate outside Bayreuth.

After Wagner's death in 1883, direction of the festival went to his wife, Cosima. Continuing the traditions her husband had begun, Cosima was a strict disciplinarian. No one sang unless she approved, and, as Lillian Nordica recalled, rehearsal at Bayreuth was like military training. Performers were expected to spend six weeks preparing their roles, and each day bulletins were delivered outlining a singer's schedule for the next day. More than general guidelines, these schedules listed when and with whom a performer was to study, and even who was to dine with the Wagner family.

Emma never performed at Bayreuth, perhaps because the six weeks of required rehearsal time was not available in her heavy schedule of performances. Polish tenor Jean de Reszke, who was highly acclaimed for his Wagnerian roles, never appeared there for neither he nor his brother Edouard could spare the six weeks. Also, the Princess of Wales, who detested Kaiser Wilhelm half-jokingly asked them not to sing

Jean de Reszke, the Polish tenor, well known for his Wagnerian and French roles

in Germany. Being the gentlemen and singing sometimes at Covent Garden, the brothers complied.

Born into a wealthy Polish family, Jean de Reszke began as baritone, enjoying only modest success early in his career. After his teacher persuaded him to train as a tenor, he made an unsuccessful return to the operatic stage. For a while, he gave only concerts, but eventually returned to the opera. From 1884 to 1889, he was the principal tenor at the Paris opera. When he first sang Wagnerian roles, his career soared. Tall, handsome, always gracious, Jean was as popular as the prima donnas were. For many, he was the ideal Lohengrin and Tristan, setting standards for all subsequent performers of the roles.

Given their respective popularity in Wagnerian roles, Emma and Jean were soon singing together. Their collaboration resulted in some of the finest performances of Wagner ever presented during the golden age of opera.

Today, it is almost impossible to imagine the impression of a superb operatic performance in the nineteenth century. When the opera was by Wagner, the effect could be shattering. Dozens of years after one landmark performance, one man recalled, "I remember every detail ... as though it had been last night. I don't know how I ever lived through it. I remember being afraid that I should take cold on the way home, because I was so excited, I perspired so that at the end of the opera my shirt, and even my collar and tie, were wringing wet."[8]

In 1888, Emma appeared with Jean de Reszke in *Lohengrin*. On 16 June, the performance received wonderful reviews, although at least one critic felt that Emma overshadowed the Swan Knight. Being surpassed by his leading lady was something which never happened to Jean. The only explanation on this occasion — other than Emma's outstanding talent — was that Jean was not in top form. An amulet he had worn in an earlier performance of *Aida* irritated a cat bite on his arm. During the opera, Jean was suffering from blood poisoning which would eventually require minor surgery.

Emma's Wagnerian roles even drew compliments from George Bernard Shaw. As music critic for a London newspaper, Shaw was often scathing. He was also a loyal Patti fan. But when Emma appeared with Jean in *Die Meistersinger*, he wrote, "Madame Albani is always at her sincerest — that is, her best — in playing Wagner. In the first scene of the second act she got so carried into her part that for the moment she quite looked it, and the quintet at the end was one of the happiest passages of the evening."[9]

The length and scope of Emma's career make it impossible to select one incident as her ultimate triumph, but four performances of *Tristan und Isolde* certainly marked an important high point. In 1896, she was singing with Jean de Reszke and again, the performances were magnificent. "Never before at Covent Garden has the wondrous beauty of this *scène d'amour* been so totally realized," wrote Hermann Klein. "To hear the music sung perfectly in tune was alone a treat that was well-nigh a revelation!"[10] Incredibly, both Jean and Emma were in their late forties, a time when many singers were already planning or beginning their retirement.

If Emma had never sung with de Reszke the magic of those performances might never have occurred. To approach perfection in an opera both lead soprano and lead tenor have to master their roles and be willing to work together. All too often, a fine soprano found her performance upset by a tenor's mistake. Worse, there was often fierce rivalry between the two stars, with each doing his or her utmost to upstage the other. Emma and Jean realized that teamwork was a far better approach. Taken separately, their performances were brilliant, but when they appeared together on the same stage the singing of Emma Albani and Jean de Reszke became legendary.

Yet they had their share of problems to solve. During her first rehearsal for *Tristan und Isolde* with Jean, Emma encountered some difficulties. It was not musical technique; how could it be with such consummate professionals? Instead, it was Emma's Victorian concept of morality which was obstructive. Towards the end of Act I, Isolde offers her beloved but unresponsive Tristan a cup in which her maid has secretly put a love potion. "After drinking the love potion," director Amherst Webber explained, "it is Isolde who speaks first, and as you say 'Tristan' you take a step forward, towards Tristan."

"Oh but I couldn't!" Emma protested. "I couldn't take the first step. Why that would be contrary to all my principles and training."[11] In spite of her Victorian inhibitions about a woman's place in a man's world, she played a superbly convincing Isolde.

Fittingly, the glorious performances of *Tristan und Isolde* took place during Emma's last season at Covent

Garden. A dozen years earlier in 1884, Ernest Gye had lost control of the theatre. In the six years following his father's death, Covent Garden had steadily declined, despite Ernest's efforts. "Each year the subscription grew smaller, each year one noted a stiff deterioration in that atmosphere of stately pomp and stiff exclusiveness that had so long been the peculiar social appanage of the Covent Garden season," reported Hermann Klein.[12]

Paradoxically, the German operas which Emma sang so well on the Continent helped bring about the demise of the Gye management. By 1882, both Drury Lane and Her Majesty's were presenting German opera seasons but the Covent Garden company was simply not equipped to follow suit. By the time it was able to offer fifteen German performances, in the 1884 season, it was too late. The audiences had gone elsewhere. Ernest was not as astute an observer of changing tastes as his father had been, and if rumours that she influenced her husband in managerial decision were true, neither was Emma.

The loss of Covent Garden did not mean the end of Emma's career. There was still oratorio, appearances in other London theatres and on the continent, and in 1889 an ambitious North American tour which proved Emma remained a dominant force in the operatic world.

Chapter Thirteen

Grande Dame of British Opera

From the mid-1870s until her triumphant performance with de Reszke in *Tristan und Isolde*, Emma led a busy and complex life. Like many of her contemporaries, she travelled almost continually, moving from one location to another, month after month, year after year. As well as appearances in London and the English festival towns, she toured Russia, Scandinavia, Scotland, Belgium, Holland and Monaco. In Denmark she was awarded the Order of Merit; in Berlin the Empress presented her with expensive vases from the Royal Pottery works. The Antwerpische Toonkunslenaars Vereeniging, a musical society, presented her with a badge of honour, as did L'Association des Artistes Musiciens of Brussels. And, when Emma performed at a benefit concert for victims of floods in Belgium, she was given a silver wreath which she displayed proudly in her home.

When not actually travelling there were always new roles to learn, old ones to improve, rehearsals and social functions to attend. In many ways it was like living in a public goldfish bowl. Then, as now, the public demanded more of its celebrities than of regular performers. Opera singers were scrutinized, interviewed, asked their opinions on just about everything. In addition to singing their operatic roles superbly, they were also expected to entertain audiences with amusing antics onstage and off. Often they behaved like wilful children with relentless energy. George Bernard Shaw described the aftermath of one performance Adelina Patti gave in London before leaving for South America. After singing

some pretty nonsense from Delibes *Lakmé* the comedy began. Mr. Ganz (the conductor) whilst the house was shouting and clapping uproariously, deliberately took up his baton and started Moszkowski's *Serenata in D*. After a prolonged struggle, Mr. Ganz gave up in despair, and out tripped the diva, bowing her acknowledgements in the character of a petted and delighted child. When she vanished there was more cheering than ever. Mr. Ganz threatened the *Serenata* again, but in vain.

He appealed to the sentinels of the green room, and these shook their heads amidst roars of protest from the audience, and at last, with elaborate gestures, conveyed in dumb show that they dared not, could not, would not, must not venture to approach Patti again. Mr. Ganz with well-acted desolation, went on with the *Serenata*, not one note of which was heard. Again he appealed to the sentinels; and this time they waved their hands expansively in the direction of South America, to indicate that the prima donna was already on her way thither. On this the audience showed such sudden and unexpected signs of giving in that the diva tripped out again, bowing, wafting kisses, and successfully courting fresh thunders of applause. Will not some sincere friend of Madame Patti's tell her frankly she is growing too big a girl for this sort of thing?[1]

Shaw may have thought Adelina too big a girl, but the audience did not. Just as they applauded delightedly at her seeming reluctance to return to the stage, they readily accepted the incongruity of her having a piano wheeled out before the curtain after one performance of *The Barber of Seville* at the Metropolitan Opera in New York. Still in costume, Adelina sat down and sang *Comin' thro' the Rye.* Years later, Nellie Melba would try the same type of entertainment, dressed in the nightgown she had worn as the strangled Desdemona.

Both Patti and Melba were simply trying to please their public by getting closer to them, and such attempts at physical closeness were not confined to a song or two after an opera had concluded. David Bispham recalled how Patti "invariably came to the footlights to sing her great arias regardless of the business of the stage: its occupants might do as they pleased as long as she had the undivided attention of the audience." Sometimes, though, a prima donna's misbehavior was not the result of her perceptions of the public's desires. Bispham wrote that in the closing scene of *Aida* "where she and the tenor are supposed to be immured in a tomb of stone ... Patti, who had instructed the stage manager to make her comfortable, would carefully adjust a sofa cushion which had been placed conveniently at hand ... would kick with one high-heeled Parisian

125

slipper a train around behind her, and, assisted by the tenor, would compose herself in a graceful position — and die."[2]

At least Patti more or less paid attention to what was happening on stage, but other singers did not. Nellie Melba once became so engrossed in a conversation with a chorister during a performance of *Les Huguenots* that she missed her cue. In an attempt to cover herself, she sang some musical nonsense. Instead of responding "Madame, I will go and bring my daughter," Plançon, as St. Bris, sang "Madame, I will go and tell Meyerbeer."[3] Manicelli, the conductor, had to hide his face in his music to keep from bursting into gales of laughter.

Outrageously overdone showmanship was never Emma's style, although the lack of it may have lessened her popular appeal. Thus she was never as well liked in America as Adelina Patti, even though the British audiences adored her, and chauvinistic Canadians considered her second to none. Still, she did play to her audiences. And, as usual, George Bernard Shaw had something to say about it. When Emma performed in Handel's *Messiah* in January 1889 at the Royal Albert Hall, Shaw noted there were "sitters and people standing two or three deep behind the chairs" in the shilling gallery. "These sitters and standers are the gallery vanguard, consisting of prima donna worshippers who are bent on obtaining a bird's eye view of Madame Albani."[4]

While the prima donna worshippers may have been impressed, Shaw was not. "Madame Albani altered the ending of her songs in the bad old fashion which is now happily for London, vanishing to the provinces." She was "too bent on finishing 'effectively' to finish well. However the two voices (Janet Patey was also singing that night) are grand voices, and so could not wholly miss the mark at any time."[5]

Shaw also criticized Emma's acting. In June of the same year, he saw her in *La Traviata* and "positively refused to take our eminent lyrical tragedienne seriously as an actress. What is more ... there is no denying the sort of thing that Madame Albani and her colleagues do at the Opera is beneath the notice of any intelligent student of dramatic art."[6]

As she grew older, Emma was frequently accused of overdoing her dramatic gestures and vocal embellishments. While it is possible that she altered her style over the years, it is probably that the criticisms resulted from changing tastes. Moreover, it is also quite likely that the gestures and little tricks of expression and movement which were delightful in a young debutante became ridiculous in a matronly opera veteran.

Was she as bad an actress as Shaw and others claimed? Was she really as good a singer as many thought? According to Oscar Thompson, author of *The American Singer*, Emma was a great technician, a craftswoman who not only mastered all the skills required of a singer, but also developed them to a remarkable degree. Her versatility, ability to learn a part quickly, and her excellent diction were probably enough to make her legendary. Yet she never seemed to show great enthusiasm over any music. "For all music she had equal praise, moderate, tepid."[7] But, as the same writer points out, Brahms wept when Emma sang part of his *Requiem* for him; while Gounod, Dvorak and Liszt all praised her highly.

For instance, in 1886, Emma sang the lead in Liszt's *The Legend of St. Elisabeth*. The composer was in London at the time and praised her for her performance, writing her a letter expressing his "admiration and thanks". Emma's talent, charm and professionalism made her popular with many composers. Hans von Bülow observed that she was "the most brilliant singing star of our era".[8] Czech composer Antonin Dvorak may well have agreed. In 1884, Emma sang his cantata *The Spectre's Bride*. The following year she performed the lead role of *St. Ludmilla*, an oratorio. Both works were popular and critical successes in England. In 1891, however, illness forced Emma to cancel, at the very last minute, her part in the premier performance of Dvorak's *Requiem Mass*. The critics were far from satisfied with the work, and it is easy to imagine the reticent Dvorak tracing the problem to Emma's absence. As he had observed before, she sang "divinely."[9]

Perhaps a clue to Emma's apparent apathy can be found in Jean de Reszke's method for learning a part. Like Emma, Jean was a virtuoso who demanded much of himself. In his opinion, if a new role did not make him weep upon first reading, he would never sing it well. He had to feel all the emotions evoked by the music, and feel them deeply. And then he analyzed them, took them apart, and sought an effective way to project them to the audience. By the time he was ready to perform, he no longer felt the emotions personally. He could, however call them forth in his audience without any danger of losing his voice in a paroxysm of feeling.

Johannes Brahms was moved to tears when hearing Emma Albani sing his Requiem.

Perhaps Emma went through a similar process. Singing and acting out a highly-charged dramatic role week after week for years would be exhausting enough without experiencing every nuance of love, anger, jealousy or fear. Thus a seeming indifference to the music was a form of professional protective detachment.

Emma's seeming apathy may also have been the result of her personality. As a child and young woman, she was highly emotional, bursting into tears when under too much stress. Over the years, she probably learned to hide her emotions under a veneer of reserve or just mature control. Certainly she had to learn to handle stress more effectively than through weeping spells. Every performance has an element of risk involved, opera-goers were also aware of such risks. A singer might miss a high note, and the ensuing debacle could mean the end of his or her career. Singers knew this, knew many of the people listening to them were morbidly anxious to see them fail. So the best opera stars either learned to cope or left the stage.

While Emma may have appeared cool to some in her feelings about music, most of the people she encountered found her warm and charming. One famous singer apparently remarked, "There is one soprano in the world I do *not* hate, and that is Emma Lajeunesse, whom they call Albani."[10] Coming from a member of a profession who considered jealous rivalry as essential to their careers as makeup and fine costumes, that was indeed high praise.

The affection Emma received from her colleagues may have come from her own determination to see the best in others. In her memoirs, she recalls her first engagement in Paris.

> Here, as elsewhere, since I began my career, I met with nothing but help and sympathy from my brother and sister artistes. I had heard much about the jealousies and difficulties only too rife in a theater, but I can truly assert that the sympathetic pleasure I always feel myself in the talent and success of any of my colleagues was ungrudgingly given to me by one and all, bringing sunshine into my operatic life, and lightening its inevitable work and anxieties.[11]

It would appear that by the time she reached the pinnacle of her career, Emma had developed into a *grande dame*, gracious, courteous, possessing high personal standards but willing to accept the shortcomings of others without criticism, and sometimes, with amusement. She recounts one incident when musician August Wilhelmj first tasted whiskey at an after-concert dinner in Glasgow. "Wilhelmj put three or four lumps of sugar into it, but no water. The sugar disguised the strength of the spirit, and he found it so good that he ordered a second and then a third allowance, treating them both in the same way. Result: Wilhelmj had difficulty in finding his bedroom, and he lost his train the next morning."[12]

Unfortunately, from a public relations point of view Emma's personality was almost as much a liability as an asset. Niceness, after all, rarely makes headlines, while Adelina Patti's greed and bursts of temper, or Minnie Hauk and Marie Roze's battles over dressing rooms made great copy for reporters. Emma's outstanding trait, her professionalism, was too often taken for granted.

Her colleagues were certainly aware of it, and critics frequently mentioned it in passing before going on to dissect the shortcomings of a particular performance. Yet some were sufficiently astute to ask how she managed to maintain her standards. Emma's formula was simple for she remained, throughout her professional life, a perpetual student.

"You are never content to sing the same repertoire over and over again, Madame Albani," Katherine Hale, a writer with *The Canadian Magazine* remarked during an interview.

And Emma replied simply, "You know as well as I do that there can be no standstill in art."[13]

Chapter Fourteen

Concerts in Canada

By 1889, Emma had appeared in most of the major opera houses of Europe. She had thrilled audiences in the Netherlands, France, Italy, Monaco, Scandinavia, Russia, and, of course, throughout Britain. She was forty-one, at the height of her career, firmly established in the music world. If she did not provide the delicious scandals Adelina Patti did, she could be relied upon for an excellent performance. Also, as an acknowledged favourite of Queen Victoria, who by this time was again appearing in public, Emma had become something of an institution in Britain.

Still, she was not quite as well known in the United States and Canada. At this time, Patti was making "farewell" tours across North America on an almost yearly basis, but Emma had not crossed the Atlantic in five years. While music lovers could read about her in the newspapers and magazines that arrived from England and Europe, many had never heard her, for her previous tours were limited to a few major cities. Even Montrealers had not heard her sing opera, because during her visit there in 1883, she had appeared exclusively in concert.

Between 1889 and 1891, Emma concentrated on singing for more North American audiences by touring extensively and appearing at the Metropolitan Opera in New York for a single season. It was a demanding period, when she crisscrossed Canada and the United States by rail, often in the icy time of winter. While these would not be her last North American appearances, they were the best she would ever give in the countries of her childhood. By the time she returned in 1896 and 1897, and then in the early years of the twentieth century, her vocal powers were declining. Only those who heard her earlier could fully appreciate the beauty of her voice or the incredible training and stamina that preserved its power.

The passage from England in the first weeks of 1889 was rough, so when Emma arrived in New York harbour on Monday, 21 January she was probably still recovering from seasickness. So were a number of the artists and possibly her son and husband who accompanied her. But by the middle of the week, the group boarded a train for Montreal and at Rouses Point, a New York state border town on Lake Champlain, they were met by a delegation of friends. Apparently Emma went directly to Chambly while Ernest continued on to Montreal, for one of the city's newspapers reported his arrival at the Windsor Hotel on January 24th. It is likely that young Freddy accompanied his mother to Chambly. He travelled with her frequently during his childhood, often bringing along his collection of toy trains. Emma was an affectionate mother, and perhaps spoiled her son with lavish presents, but she was careful to see that he was well-behaved. Sycophantic fans and flamboyant artistes might fuss over young Master Gye, (Master Freddy was how the press labelled him) but they were not the only people in Emma's circle of acquaintances. She also spent time with aristocrats, politicians and other influential members of society, many of whom wholeheartedly believed the Victorian adage "Children should be seen and not heard." Consequently, Freddy quickly learned appropriate social behaviour. Not surprisingly, he grew up to have a career in the British diplomatic service.

If Freddy did accompany his mother to Chambly, it is difficult not to speculate on Ernest's absence from this family reunion. Joseph Lajeunesse had left London after Emma's marriage, when control of her earnings would have gone from father to husband. Was there some conflict between the two men in Emma's life which kept them apart? Or did Ernest simply need to take care of business in Montreal before Emma's concert on Saturday?

The house on rue Martel, where Emma had lived as a child, had burned down years earlier. When her father returned to Chambly, Emma purchased a large house for him on the rue Bourgogne, close to the Chambly Basin. Surrounded by a stone fence and huge elm trees, possessing its own conservatory, the impressive building was promptly christened Villa Albani. When Emma visited there, she slept until after noon. Following breakfast in bed, she would dress in her finest clothes, adorn herself with jewels, including the pearl cross Queen Victoria had given her, then finally appear around three o'clock to greet the many visitors who came to call. Her spectacular attire was as much to please the visitors as herself, for she was no longer little Emma Lajeunesse but the great Madame Albani. Friends, relatives and acquaintances fortunate enough to meet her expected her to look the part.

Few were disappointed. Emma's stately, almost regal appearance added to the impression she created with designer gowns and fabulous jewels. Although she had never been precisely beautiful, as a young woman she was quite pretty. Despite the rigours of performing and travelling, she had gained some weight over the years, but this added rather than detracted from her appearance, according to contemporary tastes. Her complexion was flawless (sometimes enhanced by the judicious application of cosmetics) and her exquisite manners also helped sustain the impression that here was someone exceptional, almost aristocratic.

A reporter with the *Hamilton Spectator* described how she looked in February 1889. "The prima donna is what you would call a good-looking rather than a handsome woman with a frank and winning face that has in it all the bloom and freshness of a youthful English matron. In fact, but for her slight accent, Albani might pass as such. Her manner is singularly gracious, and her face beams with kindness and interest as she talks." Another writer described her as tall, but this could have resulted from the superb carriage of a stage performer, or may have been an illusion created by Emma's larger-than-life reputation. By contrast, the *Spectator* reporter found Ernest Gye "a short, middle-aged English gentleman with brown, closely-cropped beard and a pleasant, business-like manner."[1]

The Canadian section of Emma's tour in 1889 called for appearances in the major cities of Quebec and Ontario. As she travelled to Quebec City, Ottawa, Toronto, Hamilton and London, Emma must have noticed the many changes which had occurred since her childhood. Confederation, of course, was a major development. It was the railroads, rather than the politics, which had really changed the country.

Emma's personal interest in politics may have been casual, but she could not avoid it entirely when she was frequently in the company of the most influential politicians of the day. After concerts in Montreal and a visit to the gargantuan, electrically-lit ice palace there, the performers travelled to Quebec City. Here, Emma met the provincial premier and other notables at a luncheon, and was invited to watch a session of

Parliament. When she did, she was somewhat embarrassed when one member mentioned her presence in the house.

The Quebec City snowshoe clubs turned out in full force to greet Emma, just as their Montreal counterparts had years earlier. Two hundred young men, wearing "suits made of very thick white blanket adorned with facings and ribbons of various colours, according to the club" arrived at Emma's hotel, torches in hand, to escort her sleigh to the provincial parliament building. From a vantage point inside, she was treated to a display of fireworks.

Returning to Montreal before going to Ottawa, Emma was given the use of William Van Horne's private railway car. Van Horne was a Yankee businessman, an Illinois-born railway man who renounced his American citizenship when he joined the management of the CPR. His task was monumental: save the troubled organization from the brink of bankruptcy and complete the transcontinental line. With a combination of creative genius, hard-driving energy and sheer ruthlessness, Van Horne accomplished his goal in record time. But he was no philistine, no stereotypical railway magnate with little on his mind but profit. Interestingly, Van Horne seemed typical of an earlier age — the Renaissance. An accomplished painter and art lover, owner of one of the finest collections of Japanese porcelains on the continent, Van Horne loved beauty and appreciated comfort. Thus some of the most prominent cultural figures of the day dined with him, including Pauline Johnson and Rudyard Kipling. Putting his car at Emma's disposal was more than a gesture designed to get the railway good publicity. As a superb singer, the best singer Canada had produced, Emma deserved the finest, and Van Horne would make certain she enjoyed the best he could provide.

Emma and Ernest were invited to stay with the prime minister, Sir John A. Macdonald and his wife while in Ottawa. Then apparently their arrival plans were changed at the last minute. Ernest sent a wire advising the prime minister of their new arrival time, but the boy entrusted with the message did not deliver it until too late, and Sir John and Lady Macdonald were made to postpone their hospitality. In an abject letter of apology, C.H. Myers, the local telegraph office manager, explained what had happened, adding that the delivery boy had been fired for his dereliction of duty.

In any case, when Emma and Ernest arrived, they were greeted cordially and made comfortable at Earnscliffe, Macdonald's attractive limestone mansion on Sussex Drive and overlooking the wide Ottawa River. (Now it is used as the official residence of the British High Commissioner to Canada.) During Emma's stay, the Macdonalds hosted a reception for her, inviting "everybody in Ottawa who was anybody, and particularly those whom they thought I should like to meet. I believe I had to shake hands with something like five hundred people."[2]

In contrast to such formality, one night in the nation's capital Ernest got a close look at Canadian winter sports. In the middle of dinner, Sir John excused himself, asking Ernest to accompany him on a short outing. A new ice slide was just being opened and Sir John had promised to attend. While their wives entertained a few dinner guests and Emma worried, Sir John and Ernest drove along the river, hopped onto separate toboggans, and inaugurated the slide.

One of the people Emma met in Ottawa was Wilfrid Laurier, then a prominent member of the Liberal party. An eloquent speaker who as well as Macdonald opposed party divisions based on language or religion, Laurier was popular with both English and French Canadians. He would eventually become the country's first French-Canadian prime minister. Emma, who would meet him several times in Canada and Britain, was very impressed with Laurier.

The rebellion in the northwest and outbreaks of anti-Catholic violence instigated by Orangemen focussed Canadians' attention on the conflicts which existed between the country's main religious and linguistic groups. As an international celebrity, a French-Canadian who lived in England, Emma was often questioned about her views on French and English Canada. She told a Hamilton reporter in February 1889 that the people of Quebec "are not like the modern French people at all. They are the French of the time of Louis XIV, and they have all the old customs and usages, and even the language of that time, though the educated class are becoming quite Parisian. But the people themselves have not progressed in unison with the French — they have stood still, and it is just as well, I think."[3]

Twenty years later, in her autobiography, she was somewhat more reflective. By this time, Laurier was prime minister, and Emma wrote,

Remembering that the English conquered the French in Canada, it has always struck me as curious that a French-Canadian should be Premier and be liked by both sides. I believe the harmony that exists between the two nations is due in great measure to the absolute liberty allowed the French-Canadians by their English brethren. Their religion is not interfered with, nor their schools, and they are on a par in everything with the English, and have equal rights.[4]

In the final analysis, Emma's loyalties were with her people. "I have married an Englishman, and have made my home in England, but I still remain at heart a French-Canadian."

While she was in Ottawa, a rumour began that Emma had lived there between the ages of seven and twelve. The *Ottawa Journal* published a story which was reprinted in the Hamilton *Spectator* almost immediately.

Mr. Lajeunesse taught the choir of St. Andrews church, on a piano owned by the late Mrs. John McCarthy, and which is now in the possession of her daughter, Mrs. Alex. Duff. This piano is said to have been the only one in the city at that time, although there were plenty of instruments soon afterwards. In itself the piano was quite a curiosity. It had been in the McCarthy family for a very long time. Thirty years ago it was considered quite old. In appearance it certainly is venerable. It stands on six legs, and has drawers underneath like a sewing machine. Most of the keys are broken, and the instrument gives forth a note which is a cross between a frog croak and a fog horn. It has had an eventful history, having escaped two fires and fallen down a flight of stairs. It was on this piano that Madam Albani got her first music lesson. Madam Albani, on her recent return to Ottawa, remembered the piano and hunted it up. She has announced her intention of visiting Mrs. Duff when she returns to the city, and to run her fingers once more over the keys.[5]

This was a charming story, but totally fictitious. Obviously Mrs. Duff wanted to bask in Emma's reflected glory, now that Emma Albani was world famous. If Joseph Lajeunesse had wished to pursue his career in Upper Canada, he would certainly have chosen either Toronto or Hamilton. In the 1850s and '60s both cities offered wider opportunities for his and Emma's musical talents than this remote lumber town that suddenly became the new national capital.

From Ottawa, Emma's group went on to Toronto, which she said reminded her of "an American city — but perhaps they would not like me to say that." As usual, Emma pleased her audiences in Toronto, and in Hamilton, where she appeared next. While other members of the company went to see Niagara Falls, Emma answered a reporter's questions in her hotel room. One of them focussed on Italian versus German opera. Citing a recent article in which Lilli Lehmann claimed Italian opera was dead and no singer of the Italian school was capable of singing Wagner, the reporter asked for Emma's opinion.

"The Italian school of singing is the only school," she told him. "There is no doubt of that. An Italian singer can sing any music. Others, like the German, when they have learnt it can only sing their own music, but with the Italian it is altogether different. We, having once mastered the method, can sing anything in the world."[6] While that may not have been strictly true — or maybe Adelina Patti had simply failed to master the Italian method as completely as Emma — it did apply in Albani's case.

After Hamilton, Emma went to London, Ontario, then back to Toronto, Ottawa and Montreal for more concerts before leaving Canada for the United States and the second part of her North American tour.

She crossed the U.S. in a zig-zag travel pattern, giving concerts in several major cities and stopping in dozens of small towns along the way. Although bored by the long desolate stretches of prairie, she liked Salt Lake City and was fascinated by the acoustics of the Mormon Tabernacle. Also she loved San Francisco ... "roses in full bloom (in April) in the open air and fresh strawberries and raspberries served at breakfast. (I love raspberries)."[7] After San Francisco, she made a brief appearance in Denver, then travelled directly to New York and England.

Luigi Arditi, famous Italian conductor

Chapter Fifteen

American Touring Company

Emma returned to the United States in December 1889. Then as now, entertainers were often enlisted to help at fund-raising events, and soon after she arrived in New York the *Herald* invited Emma to sing at a Christmas dinner for its newsboys. About four hundred street vendors showed up for meat pie and vegetables at a large city restaurant. While they ate, Emma sang and accompanied herself on a piano placed in the centre of the room.

"Whilst I was singing," she recalled, "I noticed a small boy sitting quite near and staring intently at me, quite neglecting a large plate full of meat pie and vegetables which was set before him. One of the ladies attending on the little guests said to him, 'But, my boy, why don't you eat your dinner?' to which he replied, still gazing at me, 'I can't eat — I've got enough.'"[1]

Following the benefit, Emma joined the Abbey-Grau touring company. Henry Abbey and Maurice Grau had gone to considerable trouble to assemble a fine operatic touring company for the winter of 1889-1890. Abbey, an Ohio-born impresario, had been the first manager of the Metropolitan Opera in New York. Despite his extensive experience in managing such actors as Edwin Booth and Sarah Bernhardt, and the brilliant company he engaged for the first season, the Metropolitan lost money and Abbey was replaced. Undefeated, he continued to bring dramatic and musical artists to North America. Eventually, between 1891 and his untimely death at the age of 50 in 1896, Abbey would manage the Metropolitan again, this time in partnership with Maurice Grau.

Born in Moravia but raised in the United States, Grau had also managed varius musical and dramatic stars. He was one of the first American impresarios to present operas in the original language, and also had extremely high standards. With two obviously capable men in charge, the North American tour looked promising, and the potential for success was further borne out by the artists engaged by Abbey and Grau.

Thus Emma was to travel with some very dramatic personalities.

In the late nineteenth century, the membership of any touring company often read like a *Who's Who* of the music world, but the Abbey-Grau company was truly outstanding. The celebrated list of artists included, as well as Emma Albani, Adelina Patti, Lillian Nordica, Sofia Scalchi, Francesco Tamagno, Luigi Ravelli and Giuseppe Del Puente, under the direction of Luigi Arditi. In addition to an orchestra, chorus and company of dancers, the entourage was made even larger by the inclusion of various relatives and employees of the artists, including Ernest Gye, Patti's husband Ernest Nicolini, and Virginia Arditi, wife of the conductor. Together they comprised a fascinating group.

Madame Arditi was a southern belle, an American from Richmond, Virginia, whose lively letters to her married daughter provide a vivid description of the events of the tour. Her husband, Luigi, was a Piedmontese, a witty and convivial musician who was extremely well-liked by both audiences and artists. Part of Luigi Arditi's charm was his ability to laugh at himself. In his *Reminiscences*, he tells of an encounter at London's Crystal Palace with an elderly woman who bowed very low, complimenting him profusely on his music. Arditi was polite, but confused, and as the old woman walked away turned to his wife asking, "Who is it?" Laughing, Virginia informed him it was their cook.

Although Arditi had travelled widely, and like most performers, learned several languages, he spoke none of them perfectly. In Mexico, when his wife asked him to give directions to a chambermaid, he complied — in English — until Virginia pointed out that he was not as he thought, speaking Spanish. Another time, when the scheduled soprano was unable to appear at a performance, he caught sight of Mademoiselle de Lido, a young Russian singer, sitting in the audience. He rushed to her box with a request for assistance. At first she was reluctant. "How can I sing? I am not dressed!" she protested. Eventually, Arditi convinced her. Whereupon he introduced her: "Ladies and gentlemen, I am happy to say that although Mademoiselle de Lido has nothing on, she has kindly consented to sing."[2]

His occasional mangling of the language and forgetfulness did not disguise Arditi's sharp wits. After conducting an

American concert, he went to cash a cheque, but could not produce identification. "Don't you know me?" he said to the clerk. "I am Signor Arditi." The clerk remained uncertain. "Do you ever go to the opera?" Arditi demanded. "Yes, often." The conductor turned his back, lifted his hat, and pointed out his gleaming bald head. "Do you know me now?" "Oh yes. Now I know that you are Signor Arditi; it's all right. Here's the money."[3]

Arditi's light, humourous touch would smooth over many emotional tempests during the tour, for the members of the troupe, while very talented, were also extremely temperamental.

Probably, Luigi Ravelli was the most volatile of all. A small, dark man, Ravelli had been one of Mapleson's chance discoveries. Finding he needed a tenor at short notice, Mapleson learned from the hall porter that a singer had been loitering around the stage door for several days. Mapleson went out to find him, and after some nonchalant negotiations in which each man tried to appear less desperate than the other, Mapleson engaged Ravelli, to his everlasting regret.

Not that Ravelli lacked talent, but his demands often drove his associates to distraction. In *Il Rinnegato*, a now-forgotten opera by Baron Orczy, there is a sharp departure from operatic tradition when the baritone kills the tenor in a duel. The idea of such a plot shocked Ravelli for usually the tenor is the hero. Why should his appearance on stage be cut short by such a ridiculous innovation? He wanted to kill the baritone and have an expected story. When Mapleson insisted the opera be performed as written, Ravelli screamed, swore, threatened to kill the baritone and the entire cast, then finally allowed himself to be persuaded to cooperate. He would die on stage, providing he was immediately carried away by six attendants. However, Baron Orczy's opera called for the soprano to weep over the body of her beloved. Mapleson agreed to Ravelli's terms, nevertheless, until the night of the opera. No attendants appeared, and the tenor had to lie perfectly still, seething inwardly, in full view of the audience for ten minutes.

Also Ravelli's violent temper flared during a performance of *Carmen*. The title role was sung by Minnie Hauk, a soprano who despised Ravelli almost as much as he hated her. At one point, Hauk hugged him so tightly that he not only missed a high note, but lost all the buttons on his waistcoat.

141

When he shouted at her to let him go, the audience thought this was a fine bit of improvisation. But she refused, so he threatened to kill her. She was so upset that legal proceedings were instituted, and Ravelli was placed under a peace bond.

More talented and infinitely more controlled than Ravelli was the starring tenor of the troupe, Francesco Tamagno. An Italian whose reputation led to a successful tour of South America, Tamagno had been chosen by Verdi and his librettist, Boito, to create the title role of *Otello*. The premiere at La Scala in February 1887 was an unparalleled success, as much the result of Tamagno's singing and acting ability as the composer's music.

Although generally well-behaved and cheerful, Tamagno was supremely conscious of his own worth. If he wanted something, he would struggle to achieve it, and was rarely satisfied with anything less. "He didn't exactly want the earth," commented Maurice Mayer, Abbey's advance man, after discussing a contract with Tamagno, "but just about everything on it."[4] Once a contract was signed, however, Tamagno honoured it.

What a contrast Tamagno was to Adelina Patti, the reigning queen of song, who was the star attraction of the troupe! As usual, she was accompanied by her husband, Ernest Nicolini. By this time, Nicolini had more or less retired from the stage, and spent his time seeing to his wife's needs, acting as an intermediary in her frequent disagreements with managers. He had been known to measure the letters on posters when he suspected Adelina was getting a smaller billing than her contract stated, and his presence must have been just one more irritation the managers had to cope with on the tour.

Of course not all the artists would deliberately cause trouble. Most behaved professionally; however, Abbey, Grau and Arditi all knew the performers' reputations and some of the problems they had caused in the past. Sofia Scalchi, for instance, the company's lead contralto, was always businesslike in her dealings. A mediocre actress but an excellent singer, she could be relied upon to give an excellent performance most of the time. Sometimes, though, events conspired against her. Once, when asked to replace another artist, she had to refuse, claiming she had just finished a huge plate of macaroni and simply could not sing on a full stomach. Also she failed to

Francesco Tamagno, the Italian tenor known for his dramatics

appear when her pet parrot died in the middle of another tour as she was simply too distraught to go on stage.

Another example was Lillian Nordica, an American born prima donna at the beginning of what would be a long and illustrious career. Born Lillian Norton in Farmington, Maine, she was stubborn and ambitious, and was not friendly with Adelina Patti, the company's star. The "Yankee Diva" as she was called also adored sumptuous costumes, so when news of the troupe's arrival was first announced in Chicago, someone wryly remarked "Patti is bringing her voice and Nordica her wardrobe."[5] It was rumoured that Nordica had spent over £2000 on costumes from Worth, the dress designer for the Parisian elite.

With thousands of miles to tour, reputations to maintain and a definite schedule to keep, the operatic troupe had to travel the fastest and most luxurious way possible, which meant by train. Since every operatic manager had some experience with the vagaries of normal train schedules, a special train was the obvious answer. The train assembled for the Abbey tour was something of a modern marvel. There were thirteen cars in all, four baggage cars to hold the wardrobes including costumes and props but not including scenery which was contrived from whatever could be obtained locally. The baggage could have been greatly reduced if performers shared costumes as they occasionally shared roles, but that was unthinkable. No prima donna would ever wear something one of her rivals had used. There was also a dining car, Pullman cars, tourist sleepers and a coach, with the Pullmans reserved for the best artists.

"On first entering the train," wrote Virginia Arditi, "I was immensely struck by the elegance of the interior of the state saloon, and the beautiful fittings of inlaid cedar wood, but when one came to inspect the sleeping accommodations, I longed for an English first-class carriage."[6]

Tamagno and soprano, Valda, were the only artists who had private compartments. Everyone else was "expected to manage as best we could and the *best* was very uncomfortable for everybody."

As the leading tenor, Tamagno was naturally entitled to a private compartment. Why Valda, who never achieved the celebrity of Albani, Nordica or Scalchi, got her own compartment is a mystery. Perhaps the artists drew lots, or Emma and

144

Sofia Scalchi were merely being gracious. Although by the time she joined the company in Chicago it was too late to do anything, certainly Lillian Nordica must have been upset about it. She was furious that Adelina Patti had her own private car. When word of her anger reached Henry Abbey, he said he would be perfectly willing to give the singer an entire train — providing she paid for it herself. By 1901, when Nordica was at the pinnacle of her career, she did have her own car, *The Brunnhilde.*

The popular Adelina had used her private car for several years. It was a condition of her contract, just as were the six or more servants in her entourage, including a personal cook, whose salaries were paid by the company. The car, emblazoned with the diva's name, was a study in opulence. The walls and ceilings were gilded leather, decorated with Patti's monogram, pictures of flowers and musical instruments, and set off by curtains of heavy damask silk. All the fittings, lamps, tables and fine furniture were equally luxurious. The parlor had sofas and chairs upholstered in pale blue plush, while the wood panelled bedroom held a brass bed. There were electric lights, a bathtub, and even a grand piano valued at $2500, which was mounted on springs so that it remained balanced. This was Patti's home between her luxurious Welsh castle, Craig-y-Nos, and expensive hotel suites, and contained many of her favorite possessions, including her pet parrot. The bird, it was rumoured, had been trained to squawk, "Cash! Cash!" whenever Henry Mapleson entered the car.

When Adelina was not in residence, people on route were sometimes treated to tours of her car, and Chicagoans may have received a glimpse on this tour, for Adelina did not arrive with the tour train. She and Nordica joined the troupe early in December and settled at one of the local hotels. The company's engagements were scheduled from 9 December to 4 January, with Emma, Patti and Nordica alternately singing lead roles. The very first engagement was the opening of the Chicago Auditorium, a costly structure of brown granite and marble.

As usual, Patti did her spotlight-getting routine. First of all, she was the sole artist scheduled to sing at the dedication ceremonies of the "Parthenon of Modern Civilization" as one newspaper named the Auditorium. Secondly she had changed her hair colour, a drastic move. "Patti is a Blond" the headlines screamed. Actually, her hair was auburn, the result of liberal applications of peroxide in preparation for her role in *Roméo et Juliette.*

The scandalous change of hair colour was soon overshadowed by the dedication ceremony. Eight thousand people crowded into the thousand seat auditorium, while perhaps 30,000 more thronged the streets outside. Various local dignitaries made speeches, and Benjamin Harrison, President of the United States, was also on hand. "Only the voice of the immortal singer can bring from these arches those echoes which will tell us the true purpose of their construction," he said.[7]

Then Adelina appeared, wearing a gown of white brocade trimmed with black satin stripes, metal spangles and a dazzling array of pearls and diamonds. She had been contracted to sing one song, *Home, Sweet Home,* for the astronomical sum of £800. After a tumultuous ovation, however, she obliged with a second song, but that was as far as her generosity extended.

The Chicago engagement continued through Christmas and New Year, so some of the artists must certainly have longed for home and family. Patti was in mourning for her sister, Carlotta, who had died the previous summer. Like Adelina, Carlotta had a fine voice, but lameness kept her off the stage most of the time. Lillian Nordica undoubtedly missed her mother, who had been her travelling companion in the early days of her career. Then Emma and Ernest, longing for home, invited the Arditis to Christmas dinner. "How nice it will be to be in the company of friends whose sympathies are so thoroughly English as theirs!" Virginia Arditi wrote her daughter.[8] The Christmas dinner must have been a pleasant one, for Emma and Ernest made it as much like home as they could, complete with a Christmas pudding that had been packed in a basket before leaving England.

Emma appeared in four operas during the Chicago engagement, two before and two after Christmas. One of those appearances was a direct result of Adelina Patti's temperament. Almost everyone in the company had been ill with influenza, or, as they called it "la grippe". Tamagno, his throat wrapped in flannel, kept to his hotel room, while Nordica was in bed with a bad cough. Most of the other artists were just recovering or just beginning with various symptoms, prompting the auditorium manager Milward Adams to observe,

146

"Only Patti and myself are left, and I am not feeling any too well." Then disaster struck. Patti sent word she could not appear.

A delegation from the Auditorium called on the prima donna, who was sitting in her hotel parlour before a coal fire. "You are well, are you not?" Adams asked. Between bites of marshmallows, which she claimed were good for her throat, Adelina nodded. "Perfectly." "Then you can sing tonight?" "For four thousand dollars."[9] Her usual fee was $3500 plus 10% of the box office sales. One wonders if the parrot screamed "Cash! Cash!," in the background as the defeated committee slunk back to the Auditorium.

Everyone was upset and worried. Furious, Adams even kicked a man who had the audacity to ask for a free pass. Finally, the organizers approached Emma, who graciously consented to step in and perform *Les Huguenots*.

Emma's last Chicago performance, on 2 January, was also her finest. Tamagno, who had not quite recovered from his illness, got out of his bed to take the lead in *Otello*, the part which had been created for him barely two years earlier in Milan. A big man with curly brown hair and beard, Tamagno darkened his face and hands for the role. His costume was a velvet jacket and loose-fitting knee breeches; Emma, as Desdemona, appeared in an elaborately appliquéd gown, a pocket book dangling from her waist and Juliet cap on her head.

"I can never forget his whole realisation of the part, which I think one of the best I have ever seen by an artist. His physique was specially adapted to the character, and his splendid voice and temperament, combined with a wonderful amount of sympathy, made his performance of *Otello* a most remarkable one."[10]

Otello's character might have been tailor-made for Tamagno. A simple, rather unsophisticated man who collected butterflies as a hobby, he fully comprehended the predicament of the uncomplicated Moor of Venice, full of pride and passion, who found himself at the mercy of the cunningly vindictive Iago. Tamagno had also seen the play performed, with Italian tragedian Tomasso Salvini in the title role.

Tamagno threw himself wholeheartedly into the part, greatly frightening Emma. "In the last act, where he kills Desdemona, he was so apparently real that at first he made me quite nervous that he might make a mistake and forget that he was only acting."[11] Fortunately, Tamagno did not forget. The audience was thrilled.

As a souvenir of her first performance in the opera under Luigi Arditi's direction, a grateful Emma presented him with a ruby and diamond pin. "She gave it to him in such a sweet manner that we felt it really came straight from her heart," Virginia wrote.[12] Two nights later, the final appearance in Chicago took place. Then the company boarded the train once more, en route for Mexico.

Chapter Sixteen

Mexican Tour
and New York Met

The train proceeded to St. Louis on the track that followed the Mississippi River for a while. After the cold of Chicago, the warm southern climate must have been a welcome change. At Eagles, a Texas frontier town, the train was greeted by a brass band, along with a crowd of Mexican men, women and children who swarmed around the cars, gaping curiously at its inhabitants who, just as curiously, stared back at them.

Glimpses of the Mexicans and the barren landscape were almost the only amusements for the passengers. At one stop, they tried to find some amusement playing in the desert sand, but it was too hot to be comfortable. Now the heat, the length of the journey and the lack of good food put everyone into bad temper. Emma complained that the restaurant car was badly stocked and the meals were poor fare, a far cry from the luxury the railway line had promised. Occasionally, Patti sent special dishes created by her cook to one or another of the group, but having to accept Patti's concept of *noblesse oblige* must have made the food nearly indigestible for some of her rivals.

The train left Chicago on Monday. Then by Wednesday, the artists were grumbling about the food and heat, but complaints stopped abruptly when the train halted before a broken bridge. The previous Sunday, the bridge had collapsed as another train crossed it, sending the engine and cars to the bottom of a ravine. While no one was injured, the performers must have reflected on what might have been their fate when they heard the news. Momentarily, the bad food and heat were forgotten.

After a long day's wait while a temporary bridge was completed, the train proceeded. Almost immediately, it encountered more trouble as one of the Pullman cars detached from the others and was almost crushed. While the dining car

149

waiters jumped into the fields and ran for their lives, someone had the presence of mind to pull the emergency brake and no one was hurt.

By this time, the troupe's nerves must have been shattered. Most of them had done a fair amount of travelling, and undoubtedly realized how dangerous trains could be, particularly in the United States. In that year, 1890, there would be 10,000 deaths and 80,000 serious injuries from train mishaps in the United States, five times the rate in Britain. Mishaps and tragedies were always happening with early American railroads: trestles broke, tracks washed away, boilers exploded, or careless signal men and engineers gambled with passengers' lives and often lost. The fatality rate was so high, in fact, that one contemporary woodcut depicted a skeleton travelling among the regular passengers on a train.

Emma and the others looked forward to the arrival in Mexico City as a welcome respite from the tedious journey. A band met them at the station, then the company moved to the hotel which had once been a convent. Set in a grove of orange and palm trees, surrounded by a spacious verandah, the hotel looked inviting, and the management had taken great trouble to prepare for the arrival of the singers. To honour Adelina Patti, some of the best pieces of furniture had been moved from other rooms to her suite, which must have upset her rivals dreadfully. Then, as a special compliment, all the servants were ordered to take a bath.

But there was no food at the hotel, so the performers either had to eat in restaurants or have food brought in. Although it had several drawbacks, Emma and Ernest chose the latter option. The meals were "brought by a dirty young waiter with a shock head and in his shirt sleeves." Invariably, the food was cold or something had been forgotten. And rather than improving, the service actually deteriorated during the month Emma was in town. "The waiter excelled all his previous deeds when he brought up our last breakfast by letting the tray fall on the stone stairs and smashing everything on it. It made such a clatter that some people in the hotel thought that a revolution had broken out."[1]

Emma enjoyed the daytime warmth of Mexico, but she hated the cold hotel room. There was no fireplace, so to keep warm she and Ernest bought an oil stove and piled on railway rugs. During the day, they accompanied other members of the troupe on sightseeing expeditions. Virginia Arditi described visits to the Cathedral, Chapultepec, Emperor Maximilian's palace, and other points of interest. On one outing, they drove to Toluca to visit the governor. While Emma had been impressed by Mexican society and its historic structures, she was not happy about the natives, whom she considered primitive and lazy, "lounging in the sun, doing nothing all day, and when the sun goes to bed they go too."

The problems with keeping warm and well-fed were more than compensated for by the warm welcome given the performers in Mexico. It could have been a disastrous sojourn, for, a few years earlier, a man posing as Abbey's agent had sold tickets to operas then absconded with the funds. But so great was the Mexican longing for fine music that the tickets to the performance sold very quickly. "We were told that the ladies sold or pawned their jewels and pianos, and the young men went without a good dinner for a month in order to buy tickets for the opera."[2] Virginia Arditi heard of one woman who paid £30 for a box and £14 for two seats for her maid and her husband's valet.

The Mexicans may have been enthusiastic, but they were also an extremely demanding audience, "more *exigeant* than an Italian audience," Virginia Arditi claimed.[3] When *Faust* was produced, Ravelli was out of voice, and the ticket holders hissed him. Novara never had a hand during his entire performance, and the only time Emma was applauded was when she sang alone.

However, Tamagno was an instant success, although the audience might have been a little confused had they known what was really going on behind the scenes. The tenor insisted that, for dramatic effect he had to climb up to Desdemona's elevated bed in the last act. One of his histrionic embellishments in the role of Otello was to roll down the stairs after stabbing himself in remorse for killing his innocent wife. He could hardly do that without the steps, and would not be persuaded to change his acting methods. With steps but no platform available, he found four strong men who knelt down on their hands and knees while the bed was supported on their backs. Emma was dreadfully anxious during the last segment of the opera, convinced that the men and then the bed would collapse. "It was a very ridiculous position for a prima donna in a very dramatic situation."[4]

Still, travelling performers were accustomed to improvising. In Denver the previous year, opera had been staged in a church, on boards covering the huge baptismal font. Poet Pauline Johnson, who travelled extensively during the same years as Emma, once had to change costumes in a grain storage bin. Also, on a subsequent trip across the Canadian prairies, Emma's company even had to borrow a locomotive lantern to provide makeshift moonlight in the garden scene of *Faust*.

The Mexican engagement, which had been originally scheduled for two weeks, was prolonged to nearly three weeks when an engagement in Los Angeles was cancelled. The three extra performances the company gave did not increase profits, though, since most of the opera lovers had already spent most of their money. Nevertheless, it was a lucrative engagement. After fifteen performances, the group had earned over £40,000.

California was the next destination, and again the journey was filled with perils. Spring floods sent water roaring down mountainsides, and the train was often forced to stop until the water subsided or the rails were repaired. The dangers and problems of train travel could have been worse. For ten days in January, snow completely isolated San Francisco from the outside world. Fortunately, the blockade was broken in time for the troupe's arrival, and the welcome they received in San Francisco more than compensated for the inconveniences of the trip. Emma was "much delighted to get into the beautiful Palace Hotel after so much discomfort and inferior food in Mexico and on the train."[5]

She enjoyed San Francisco, finding the climate agreeable and many of the people warm and pleasant. However, what she called the lower classes were "rather lawless". Some eager music lovers got into the theatre gratis by climbing a ladder to a window in the gallery. A policeman was posted at the window to turn them back, but he saw no reason to deprive such dedicated enthusiasts of their chance to hear fine opera. He simply charged them the regular admittance and pocketed the proceeds!

The San Francisco audiences were much easier to please than the Mexicans had been and there was much to see and do. Various members of the group rode cable cars to see Cliff House, sailed to a huge shoreside boulder where seals gathered, or to visit Chinatown. Of course, there was the

Golden Gate Bridge, which even then was a major tourist attraction.

After twelve days in San Francisco, the troup travelled to Denver, Omaha, Louisville and back to Chicago. During these engagements, the performers again faced the perils of travelling in winter cold. In Denver, the audience wore coats and earmuffs throughout Emma's performance of *Faust*. She did not sing in Omaha, and was probably relieved to hear of what she had escaped. Lillian Nordica was one of the artists who did sing there, and she shivered through *La Traviata* at the Coliseum, which normally served as a skating rink. In Louisville, Kentucky, it was so unseasonably cold that many ticket holders simply stayed away. Those who did appear soon forgot the cold as they watched Emma and Tamagno's performance of *Otello*.

Returning to Chicago for a five-day engagement, the company found audiences had suddenly lost interest in Italian opera and were eagerly awaiting the arrival of a German opera company under the direction of Walter Damrosch. They went on to Boston, arriving, appropriately in a city with a large Irish population, on St. Patrick's Day. Emma gave two performances of *Otello* in the Mechanics' Hall, a huge auditorium normally reserved for conventions and exhibitions. It was not the most comfortable setting for an opera, and critics complained about the "penitential seats" and the distance from the stage. Nevertheless, Emma and Tamagno continued to receive curtain call after curtain call for their performances.

Singers must have found it difficult to remain poised, smiling and interested-looking as they bowed to audiences time after time, and most must have welcomed any sort of diversion. Perhaps that is why, after one matinée in Boston, Emma went over to Virginia Arditi, who always sat in the wings, whisked her chihuahua off her lap, and brought Chiquito onto the stage, to the delight of the audience.

Tour appearances in Philadelphia and New York followed. On 24 March 1890, the Abbey-Grau company opened at the Metropolitan Opera House. This was Emma's first engagement at the theatre. While avid opera buffs were more excited about the imminent appearance of Adelina Patti, Emma was the star of opening night, in the first New York City production of *Otello*.

Tamagno's creation of the role had been widely acclaimed, but, according to music critic George C. Odell, he was something of a disappointment to New York audiences. His appearance was commanding, his acting dramatic, his voice powerful, but too nasal for American tastes. Nevertheless, the opera drew fine reviews and high praise for Emma. Her "lovely singing…" was the "great treat of the evening… It is long since we have seen anything on the operatic boards more charming histrionically or more exquisite vocally than her Desdemona. Her pure clear soprano never played her false for a moment."[6]

Patti duly appeared, receiving rave reviews for *Semiramide* but somewhat subdued accolades for *La Sonnambula*. Lillian Nordica also sang, so the three sopranos alternated for the rest of March and into April. On 12 April, Patti cancelled a scheduled appearance in *La Traviata*, and Emma stepped in with a performance of *Faust*. Disappointed at the announced substitution, many ticket holders unwisely demanded refunds, for Odell reported, "those who remained heard some lovely singing by Albani."

By a curious twist of fate, the Abbey-Grau engagement ended the dominance of German opera at the Met. Just as Emma had helped to interest London audiences in Wagner, she, Patti and Nordica now stimulated a taste for Italian opera in New York.

Emma may not have had much time to reflect on the impression she and her fellow artists created for working in America was a demanding experience. In Europe, a singer might perform in the same opera night after night, but not so in the United States. Certainly the fees were higher, yet they were offset by higher expenses, travelling time, constant rehearsal for ever-changing roles and the dangers of a harsher climate. Speaking for himself and his brother, Jean de Reszke said, "Our personal enjoyment, if our engagements were abroad, would be incalculably greater."[7]

When the engagement at the Metropolitan ended, Emma and some other artists went to Albany, Toronto, Montreal and Quebec. Although she had appeared in these places in concert in the past, Emma had not sung opera in all of them. This time, she was determined to do just that.

Her return to Albany was met with the usual outpouring of public affection. As she stepped onto the balcony outside her

Emma Albani in the costume, complete with the expected purse, of Marguerite in Faust

room at the Kenmore Hotel, the band played a selection from *Tannhäuser*, and the crowd tossed their hats in the air in greeting. Emma, in a black dress, black beaded cape and black toque, smiled, blowing kisses to them, and was then escorted to a reception at the high school.

The chapel was used as an auditorium and was filled to overflowing with students and well-wishers. As she entered, everyone stood up applauding as Principal Robinson escorted her to the platform. Members of the choir were visibly unnerved in the presence of so great a singer, but relaxed as their songs drew smiles and nods of approval from Emma. Then it was the diva's turn, whose selection, predictably, was *Home, Sweet Home*. When she finished, the listeners were momentarily stunned into silence. Then their applause broke out, the loud noise nearly shaking the building. A young student, Lillian Gilligan, presented Emma with a basket of roses. Overcome with emotion, Emma was temporarily speechless. After Ernest spoke quietly to her for a moment, she recovered and sang *Robin Adair*. Finally, as the ceremony drew to a close, the choir, audience and the international star joined together in *Auld Lang Syne*.

Emma's operatic performances in Albany were excellent. A letter to the music column of the *Albany Evening Journal* said, "Never to have heard her in opera is to miss the best half of her splendid achievements." The writer then drew attention to Emma's excellent personal reputation. "She has kept her name unspotted by any kind or degree of scandal."[8]

Her return to Montreal and Quebec City was a repetition of past visits. As well as operatic performances in Montreal, she took part in a benefit for Notre-Dame Hospital on 10 May at the Victoria Rink. Six thousand people came to hear her and other French-Canadian artists, including pianist Salomon Mazurette, violinist Alfred De Sève and the Bande de la Cité conducted by Ernest Lavigne. In Quebec City there was no theatre available so Emma could only appear in concert, but was still heartily welcomed as she had been elsewhere. Along with an album of scenic Canadian views, Emma was presented with yet another poem by Louis-Honoré Fréchette.

Gifts of poetry were often made to popular singers. While they were sometimes mawkishly sentimental and poorly written, they were presented with sincere feelings. One of the most unusual ever written in Emma's honour was probably *When*

THE NEW GRAND OPERA HOUSE, TORONTO.

The New Grand Opera House on Adelaide Street West in Toronto in 1874 had a capacity of over fifteen hundred.

Albani Sang by William Henry Drummond. Drummond's "Habitant" poems were popular in late nineteenth century Canada, and are still in school text books today. To some extent they make fun of French-Canadian habitants, stereotyping them as uneducated farmers who always speak a rhythmical-type of broken English. But the poems were a reflection of that era, and they did help acquaint English-Canadians with Québécois culture, in a different way than Cornelius Krieghoff's paintings.

When Albani Sang tells the story of two habitants who travel from Chambly to Montreal to hear Emma sing. The speaker, Antoine, has never heard of her before that day, and knows little about opera, but he is astounded by "ma-dam's" singing, especially when she appears alone at the end of the programme and begins a song in French:

Dat song I will never forget me, 'twas song of de leetle bird,
W'en he's fly from it's nes' on de tree top, 'fore res' od de
    worl' get stirred,
Ma-dam she was tole us about it, den start off so quiet an'
low,
An' sing lak de bird on de morning, de poor leetle small
oiseau.

I 'member wan tam I be sleepin' jus' onder some beeg pine
tree
An' song of de robin wak' me, but robin he don't see me,
Dere's not'ing for scarin' dat bird dere, he's feel all alone on
    de worl'
Wall! Ma-dam she mus' lissen lak dat too, w'en she was de
    Chambly girl!

'Cos how could she sing dat nice chanson de sam' as de bird I
    was hear,
Till I see it de maple an' pine tree an' Richelieu ronnin' near,
Again I'm de leetle feller, lak young colt upon de spring
Dat's jus' on de way I was feel, me, w'en Ma-dam All-ba-nee
is sing!

An' affer de song it is finish, an' crowd is mak' noise wit'
    its han',
I s'pose dey be t'inkin' I'm crazy, dat mebbe I don't
onderstan',
Cos I'm set on de chair very quiet, mese'f an' poor Jeremie,
An' I see dat hees eye it was cry too, jus' sam' way it go wi't
me.

158

Dere's rosebush outside on our garden, ev'ry spring it has got
    new nes',
But only wan bluebird is buil' dere, I know her from all de
res',
An' no matter de far she be flyin' away on de winter tam,
Back to her own leetle rosebush she's comin' dere just de
sam'.

We're not beeg place on out Canton, mebbe cole on de winter,
too,
But de heart's 'Canayen' on our body, an dat's warm enough
for true!
An' we'en All-ban-ee was got lonesome for travel all roun' de
worl'
I hope she'll come home, lak de bluebird an' again be Chambly girl![9]

But Emma would never live permanently in Chambly again. Although the 1889-1890 tour was not her last in Canada and the U.S., it was the most successful. In New York, she complained to a *New York Tribune* reporter, "We have been roasted in Mexico, drenched to the skin in San Francisco, frozen to death in the western cities. We spent six days in the cars without stopping from Chicago to Mexico. It was simply horrid. But three weeks in Mexico were ample compensation for all discomfort. Mexicans do not see good opera very often, and will cheerfully pay $12 a ticket and live on bread and water."[10]

The inconvenience and dangers were many, but the tour was an unparalleled success.

A matronly Emma Albani wearing the pearl cross which Queen Victoria had given her as well as some other decorations and medals.

Chapter Seventeen

Touring the British Empire

Emma spent another season in Britain, then in late 1891 returned for a full season at the Metropolitan Opera in New York. Although her last North American tour had been under the auspices of the Metropolitan Opera, she was not a permanent member of the company. This time, however, she was hired as leading soprano at New York's newest opera house. For her debut on 23 December, she played Gilda in *Rigoletto* opposite Gianini as the Duke of Mantua and Camera in the title role.

As Henry Kreihbel pointed out in his *New York Tribune* review, *Rigoletto* had not been a great success with New York audiences, and Emma's presence did not improve things very much.

> Madame Albani is an artist who always commands respect of her earnestness and intelligence of her effort. Her wisdom in retaining the role of Gilda in her repertory is questionable. Neither in appearance nor in voice is she able longer to produce the illusion of youthfulness and emotional ardor inherent in the part. The delight which she gives comes from a recognition of her artistic knowledge and devotion rather than the sensuous charm of her singing. Last night these qualities were thrown into a bright light by contrast with the viciousness which marked the singing of all her colleagues, except the choristers...[1]

Emma had originally been scheduled to appear in *Les Huguenots* on 18 December 1891, but felt ill and was replaced by Nordica. While one of her rivals cancelled because of illness so often that she was nicknamed "the great indisposed", Emma seldom missed a performance. In a short time she recovered and appeared in *Faust, Don Giovanni, Les Huguenots* and *The Flying Dutchman*. While Tamagno had not been engaged by the Metropolitan to recreate his role in *Otello* during this season, Jean de Reszke made an admirable substitute.

It was fortunate that both Jean and Edouard, old colleagues of Emma's, were on hand during the Metropolitan season. Although Abbey and Grau had gone to great expense to assemble a stellar company, they did not devote quite so much attention to the details of production. When they announced plans to produce *Otello* they encountered some major difficulties. The stage manager was unfamiliar with the Italian opera, and neither he nor his two assistants had seen *Otello* produced. To compound the problem, one of the assistants spoke only English, the other only French. "When the three come together it is as good as a farce," remarked the ever jovial Edouard de Reszke.[2] A farce might be amusing backstage, but it would never do for audiences which enjoy grand opera, particularly if they already had a marked preference for German opera. With almost any other leading artists the problem would have deteriorated into a session of name calling and histrionic displays of temper. Instead, Emma, Jean and Edouard shared their talents and their collective powers of persuasion and rehearsed the company, with satisfactory results.

Emma most likely would have continued to perform at the Metropolitan for several years, but in August 1892 a fire broke out. Damage to the stage and auditorium was severe, and so the 1892-93 season was cancelled. By the time the Metropolitan was reopened, Emma had commitments elsewhere.

In 1896 she returned to Canada, and travelled as far west as Vancouver, stopping at several cities along the way. She marvelled at the landscape, but shuddered at an Indian jailed in the Northwest Police barracks in Calgary, "whose latest exploit was throwing a baby on to the fire. He glared at us more like a wild beast than a human being, and I rejoiced that an iron-grated door intervened between him and myself."[3]

At St. Boniface, Manitoba, she sang in the Cathedral during the Sunday Mass, evoking a complimentary speech from the archbishop.

I wish to express the satisfaction, pleasure and honour we have today in the presence of one of the Queens of the musical world — one who is a favourite of our gracious Queen. I welcome her with all the cordiality of a fellow countryman and all the satisfaction of a Catholic Bishop who is proud to

162

see his countrywoman preserving, amid the glories of the world, the old traditions of her faith and nationality. May God grant that, after a long life of success and true merit, she may everlastingly sing with the angels the praises of God.[4]

In the many remaining years of her life Emma would tour Canada a few more times.

During the 1896 tour, Adam Brown, a prominent Hamiltonian heard her in concert. He wrote to his wife in England, "I have just got back from the Albani concert. I never had such a music treat in my life — her singing was beyond description. *Ave Maria* was heavenly."[5]

The *Spectator*, while kind, was somewhat less enthusiastic.

There were many who went to hear her on Saturday night with some misgiving as to whether that wonderful voice which had thrilled the people of two continents was still able to satisfactorily meet the demands upon it. Such misgivings were warranted, and yet it would be strange if anyone were disappointed with Madam Albani's vocal performance. Her voice, it is true, has not all the freshness and purity which used to distinguish it; there are signs of wear, and in the upper register the quality is a trifle strained and the intonation uncertain. Yet the voice is as broad and full as it was of old, and it is still wielded with that superb art and fine taste which have made Albani one of the foremost artists of her time.

The reporter was not impressed by Emma's stage mannerisms, however.

The great singer retains her early juvenility of manner. Her entrance on the stage and her exit from it are as startling as ever. When she comes on she rushes forward, her arms extended as if in an impulse to embrace the entire audience, and when she retires she skips along like a kittenish miss in her teens. Even great singers are not free from the delusion that the coquettish airs which are pleasing in a young maid must also necessarily be so in a mature matron.[6]

Audiences might choose to ignore Emma's "coquettish airs" and thrill to her still-pleasing voice, but she was not drawing the audiences she once had. After the Hamilton appearance, the theatre manager revealed that although the audience was a large one the production costs had also been high and he had lost money.

Yet this was the same year in which Emma was a triumphant Isolde to Jean de Reszke's Tristan. Recordings made around 1904 or 1905 and re-released in 1967 demonstrate that, even with a marked decline in her voice she was still a wonderful singer. Perhaps by 1896 her voice was simply no longer as reliable as it had once been. Certainly the effort of singing an entire opera, especially one by Wagner, was becoming more and more taxing. At the same time, there was increasing competition from younger prima donnas such as: Emma Eames, Nellie Melba and Lillian Nordica. Reluctantly, Emma gave up the operatic career which had spanned twenty-four years. Her last operatic appearance at Covent Garden took place in 1896; her season with the Metropolitan marked the last opera she performed in the United States. However, her musical career was by no means over. She still appeared in concerts and oratorio, and because of her long list of accomplishments her reputation was secure. Her best singing days may have been over, but she continued to draw audiences. Emma had become something of a legend.

As well as continued appearances in London and other European cities, and engagements at the English music festivals, Emma went on world tours. In 1898 she sailed from Naples to Sydney, Australia, where she appeared before a crowd of 3,000. She also sang in Brisbane, Melbourne and Adelaide. In 1907, she returned to the South Pacific, this time also travelling to Tasmania and New Zealand.

Emma apparently enjoyed her food, for she often mentions it when recounting her adventures. She was delighted with the cream in New Zealand, but a little disappointed in Invercargill, when she learned that strict liquor laws made it impossible to obtain beer and wine. Fortunately, the laws were not strictly enforced and a telegram to another town soon brought a delivery of liquor by the next train.

This was an extensive tour which she embarked on in 1907. After concerts in Perth and Western Australia, she and Ernest sailed for India. The first stop was at Colombo, Ceylon, where they enjoyed the hospitality of the local governor, Sir Henry McCallam. When she crossed to Madras, India, a similar diplomatic invitation was extended, for Emma and Ernest stayed with Sir Arthur and Lady Lasley at Government House.

Emma's concerts were well-received in India, where professional English-style entertainments were rare. "I believe we had every English man and woman off duty at all our Indian concerts, and the prices were high."[7] Emma visited Bombay, Calcutta, Lahore, Delhi, Rawal Pindi, Lucknow, and, of course, Agra, site of the Taj Mahal. Everywhere she and Ernest were welcomed by the English population, meeting, among other notables, Lord Kitchener and Lord and Lady Minto. They were treated to various unusual sights and experiences, including a ride in a camel-drawn carriage. Emma found Indian exotic and fascinating, marvelling at the native costumes, but expressing a little note of disappointment. During her stay she saw "not one snake and only two elephants".[8]

Emma also toured South Africa just before the Boer War. While artists, especially if they were women, were generally not expected to make political statements, Emma made her opinion of the Kruger government very clear following her first concert in Johannesburg. Fully aware that it had been banned, she started to sing *God Save the Queen*. The predominantly English audience joined in immediately. "The police did not intervene, but I think that, if they had, the Boer War would have begun prematurely."

Her South African journey also took her to the diamond mines in Kimberley, where she was welcomed by Zulu miners. They danced for her, then one said, "Lady, please sing." Emma stood on a chair while the miners squatted around her listening to *Home, Sweet Home*. "At the end, the Zulus applauded me uproariously and accompanied me to the gate dancing and shouting like madmen."[9] In addition to her memories, Emma took home an uncut diamond as a souvenir of her visit.

In the course of her career, Emma saw almost every major city in the British Empire and many minor ones; although by the time she travelled to the far reaches of the globe, her vocal powers were declining. She was forty-four when she was engaged for the season at the Metropolitan. By the time she travelled to Australia and South Africa she was over fifty. In spite of her age, her skills, experience and the reputation she had developed over the years were still enough to thrill audiences.

165

An integral part of her legendary drawing-power was her personality. Emma was an exception to the rule that prima donnas had to behave like spoiled children. She made complaints when they were due about poor conditions, bad food, and having to shake hands with hundreds of people at a time, although she accepted the latter inconvenience as one of the responsibilities of stardom. Still, she was vain enough to send one magazine editor an autographed picture of herself as a Christmas greeting, and she definitely expected all the perquisites due a singer of her rank and experience. Once she refused to let Melba debut in "her" opera, *Rigoletto*, when Melba first appeared at Covent Garden. When Melba received unsatisfactory reviews for that performance elsewhere however, Emma, sensing no competition, allowed her to play Gilda.

Emma was also known to insist on her own idea for some interpretations of certain arias. From time to time she performed *Sull'aria*, a duet from Mozart's *Marriage of Figaro* which she had sung with Adelina Patti at the American White House. The two singers of the duet are the Countess Almaviva and her maid Susanna, and the piece is written so that at one point the maid's voice takes the higher notes, dominating that of the Countess. When Emma came to sing it with a much younger soprano, she insisted that she would take the higher notes, regardless of how the piece had been written.

On the whole, however, Emma was respected both professionally and personally and much of that respect was a direct result of her character. "Madame Albani is as charming as ever",[10] Virginia Arditi wrote to her daughter during the hectic tour of 1890-91. "Charming", "kind", "open", were words frequently used to describe Emma. "She is a handsome woman, of unbounded vivacity, and speaks with a charming French accent. She accompanies her story with constant gesture, and is always smiling. She will look at you and speak most seriously, but her eyes are ever twinkling with merriment," wrote one interviewer.[11] Another woman who read of Albani as a child, worshipped her from afar and finally met her was overwhelmed to find her "kind and gracious, as I had imagined her in my dreams."[12]

Often sentimental, easily moved to tears, Emma won many friends by her charm and acts of kindness. When she stayed at her father's house in Chambly in 1903 she made friends with a neighbour and her two little girls. With no

Emma Albani, famous for her starring roles in opera and oratorio, toured world-wide.

grandchildren of her own as Freddy had never married, Emma's affection for the girls is understandable. When she returned in 1906, she brought gifts for the girls, who were three and five by this time. The beautiful dolls Emma gave them were so expensive that their mother would not allow the girls to play with them, but the children must have been enchanted by the gifts. The older girl was Gaby Bernier, a Montreal couturière who retained memories of the queenly opera singer and her gorgeous outfits for the rest of her life.

Underneath Emma's charm was a woman with a strong character, disciplined and ambitious, but it was the charm which won friends in the most exalted social circles of five continents. And it was probably this charm as much as her singing which endeared her to the most exalted of them all, Queen Victoria.

Chapter Eighteen

Favourite of Queen Victoria

In a life as long and complicated as that of Queen Victoria, there must be many people involved. Her position brought her into contact with the most fascinating people of the world, while the blood ties of international marriages connected her to every royal family in Europe. Emma Albani was only one of many entertainers who appeared before the Queen, but the relationship which developed between the two women was in many ways unique.

Victoria had enjoyed music since childhood, and her musical education had been a thorough one. Mendelssohn was her music teacher for a time, and the operatic basso Lablache had given her singing lessons. At first, she was so awed by the singer's presence that she could not make a sound, but she eventually recovered, and developed a very nice singing voice.

As a teenager she was completely enthralled by the opera. Her idol was Giuletta Grisi, the darling of London opera lovers. Just eight years younger than the prima donna, Victoria took careful note of every aspect of the singer's dress and appearance. When her mother, the Duchess of Kent, arranged for a special concert in celebration of Victoria's sixteenth birthday, Grisi was the star attraction. The princess noted exuberantly, "Mademoiselle Giuletta Grisi ... a most beautiful singer and actress ... and likewise young and pretty ... I was *very much amused indeed.*"[1]

Victoria, in fact, was fascinated by the stage, and after her marriage spent many hours watching theatrical and operatic performances with Prince Albert. By this time Grisi's career was nearly over. Jenny Lind "who is perfection"[2] was then the most popular singer. Victoria also adored Mario, the Italian tenor, especially in his role in *Les Huguenots*. After Prince Albert died in 1861, Victoria shunned public performances, and even the state concerts at the palace. She did enjoy more private concerts, however, and her sense of duty and conviction that the arts must be encouraged were only a por-

Queen Victoria thoroughly enjoyed many types of music.

tion of the reason for her presence at concerts. Victoria simply could not live without music.

Emma's debut at Windsor Palace in July 1874 was auspicious, and as her career progressed she was often invited back. She soon learned the Queen possessed an impressive knowledge of music. "Almost every school of music appeared to appeal to Queen Victoria. Sometimes, she would ask me to sing two or three or more little French songs, one after another. Then she would suggest something by Brahms, or perhaps Grieg, or possibly Handel or Mendelssohn; and often I have concluded with some simple song that I knew she was fond of." Mendelssohn, Emma felt, especially pleased the Queen, for she would often sit enraptured, perhaps dreaming of bygone days when Albert was still alive.

She also adored Scottish songs. Victoria spent many happy weeks in Scotland during Albert's lifetime, and continued to return to the Balmoral area throughout her life. She often asked Emma to sing *The Bluebells of Scotland*, which she called the "hieland laddie song". She also liked *Annie Laurie*.

Nor was her taste limited to classical music and folksongs. Victoria once surprised several ladies of her household by selecting music and singing excerpts from a Gilbert and Sullivan operetta. The Queen had a pleasant voice, and if she sometimes forgot the words or the title to a song, she felt no hesitation in humming a few bars to explain to Emma what she wanted to hear. Of course Emma was not the only artist who entertained the Widow of Windsor, but she was a favourite. "I am anxious to recommend Madame Albani to you," Victoria wrote to the Empress of Austria. "She is my Canadian subject, an excellent person, known to me, a splendid artiste, and I take much interest in her."[3]

Because Victoria had given up going to public performances, Emma and other artists brought the latest operas to her. Gounod was one of Victoria's favourite composers, but she had never seen *Faust*, since it was not produced in London until after Albert's death. So Emma frequently sang selections from the work, either alone or with other singers, thus the Queen experienced some of the latest music.

She also enjoyed *The Golden Legend*, although Emma apparently had to coax her to listen to some of the music. "In the end, she became intensely eager to attend a performance of

Sir Arthur Sullivan's masterpiece, and though I did not venture to actually suggest it, I did endeavour indirectly to foster her desire to be present at one performance."[4] It took several months, but one morning Emma received a note from the Queen telling her that she would attend a performance of *The Golden Legend* at Albert Hall.

"The day arrived and when I came forward to sing my first solo and saw the Queen occupying the Royal box, attended by several members of the Royal Family, I think I felt more delighted than I have ever felt in my life before."[5] Victoria was so happy with the excursion that she attended other performances. In 1886, she boasted to her private secretary, Sir Henry Ponsonby, that she had already been to Albert Hall twice, "to hear Gounod's splendid music and Albani's glorious singing."[6]

Victoria was very impressed with Emma, and not only because of her music, but also because she was fond of attractive people, often recording in her diary detailed observations of their appearance and dress. When Emma first sang at Windsor, she was a pretty young woman, and as she aged she retained a great deal of her attractiveness. At the same time, her unblemished personal character must have met with the Queen's approval. Here was a singer about whom no hint of scandal had ever arisen, a respectable wife and mother who, despite her French-Canadian heritage, possessed a thoroughly English sensibility.

In 1889, Jean and Edouard de Reszke appeared at a royal concert for the first time. Apparently the Queen had heard much about them, and with her curiosity aroused, she was determined they should sing for her. When the rumour was spread that the brothers would appear at Windsor, all the prima donnas in London became flustered, wondering who would be chosen to accompany them. That Emma was selected underscores the high esteem in which she was held by her sovereign.

Jean recorded his impressions of the event in a letter to a friend. After singing the duet from *Lohengrin* with Emma, Jean sang a song from *Faust*, then Emma sang another song. Jean and Edouard presented the duet from *Carmen*, and the concert ended with a special request from the Queen that Jean and Emma sing the duet from *La Traviata*.

172

"The Queen, smiling and full of kindness, approached us and paid us many compliments."[7] Questioning the brothers in perfect French, Victoria was astonished to learn that suave and handsome Jean was older than the bulky, bearlike Edouard. "...and this discussion, in which Madame Albani was called upon to arbitrate ... greatly amused the Queen." Jean also noted the Queen was a genuine lover of music. "...one could easily see by her eyes and in the movements of the head with which she emphasized the chief passages."[8]

Recording the event in her diary, Victoria wrote, "The duet from *Lohengrin* which is quite a long scene, was beyond anything beautiful, so dramatic, and Albani almost acted it. She was in great force. The music lasted till four and I could have listened to it much longer. It was indeed a treat."[9]

Another treat for Victoria were her visits to Scotland. In the early 1850s, she and Albert bought Balmoral Castle. The original structure was too small for their growing family and retinue, so Albert remodelled it. Life at Balmoral was much more casual than in England, although one peer commented that the drawing room there was even uglier than the one at Osborne. It was a matter of "tartanitis" Lord Clarendon said — tartan curtains, carpets and furniture, with thistles almost everywhere.

Victoria and Albert both loved life in Scotland. Far from the prying eyes of their more sophisticated British subjects, they could both relax. Victoria thought nothing of creeping through the brush for hours in freezing weather to stalk a deer, or of lying in the heather to enjoy the fresh air. She frequently made unexpected visits to the local tenants, bringing gifts of food or clothing or money and giving special attention to the children. In return, the local people treated her with blunt forthrightness and courtesy.

The royal couple's fascination with Scotland helped make it something of a fashionable place to spend a vacation. In the autumn of 1883, Ernest and Emma stayed at Old Mar Lodge, thirteen miles from Balmoral.

They had been looking for a vacation house in nearby Braemar, and mentioned their search to a friend. The friend in turn spoke to Lord Fife, who owned an estate near the River Dee. Lord Fife offered his shooting lodge in the Mar Forest to Emma and her husband.

"I cannot describe the beauty of that country, nor the delightful and healthful change it was after the hard work and the turmoil of a London season,"[10] Emma wrote. She and her family spent two months there on their first visit. They often went fishing, having been given permission to do so by Lord Fife. Emma was an enthusiastic angler. "One year — I shall never forget it! — I actually caught a salmon."

Hearing that her talented Canadian subject was in the area, Victoria summoned her to sing at Balmoral. In 1884, when another invitation was issued and accepted, the Queen asked about Old Mar Lodge. She had been to the main house, Mar Lodge, about three-quarters of a mile from the place where Emma was staying. When Emma boldly invited her to visit, the Queen responded, "Well, I think I will."[11]

A few days later a telegram arrived announcing Victoria would come to call at 4:30. Emma was in a panic, but "luckily there was the wherewithal to prepare a fairly good tea ... and the Queen's kindness and thoughtfulness soon put us at our ease."[12]

Victoria relished these informal visits, which became something of an annual event. In addition, Emma was generally asked to Balmoral once or twice a season, to sing in very casual circumstances. Often, her only audience was the Queen, a lady-in-waiting, and a member of the Royal Family.

Emma must have been relieved that her audience was small on one particular occasion. "I sat down at the piano to accompany myself when alas! one of the legs of the stool broke and I rolled upon the ground at the Queen's feet. She was much concerned in case I had hurt myself, but my stage experience had taught me to tumble about without harm. When it was seen that all was right with me, the Queen laughed heartily and a fresh stool was sent for."[13]

Both the Queen's laughter and her concern for Emma were completely in character as Victoria's sense of humor was a broad sort. She loved slapstick, and thought it a great joke when one companion tumbled head over heels down a steep bank, and would have continued down another if Albert had not intervened. Yet she was inherently kind-hearted.

Although Victoria had nine children of her own, she did not like babies. "An ugly baby is a very nasty object — and the prettiest is frightful — till about four months; in short as long as they have their big body and little limbs and that terrible

" DEAR MADAME ALBANI-GYE,

" I am sending you with these lines the souvenir I spoke of when I wished you good-bye, in recollection of that charming evening of the 18th Sept., which I shall always remember with pleasure.

" Trusting that you will have a good passage, and that your health may be good and you not overtire yourself,

" Believe me always,

" Yours very sincerely,

" VICTORIA, R. I."

One of the letters of appreciation that Queen Victoria sent with gifts to Emma Albani.

froglike action."[14] Yet she enjoyed children. While Albert was alive and her own children were very young, she gave parties and children's balls for them. On one occasion, the Queen even got down on all fours to romp with the son of a lady-in-waiting.

Freddy Gye was seven years old when Victoria first visited Old Mar Lodge. A well-trained child, he was quiet and polite, but when the Queen was driving off in her carriage, Freddy turned to Emma and said, "Oh mummy, what a little woman for such a big Queen."

Dogs were also a great favourite with Queen Victoria. She was always getting new dogs, provoking one advisor to comment that she had been smothered by them. In Scotland, she visited a local church where the minister normally gave sermons while his collie lay quietly by the pulpit. If the sermon stretched too long, the dog would yawn and become restless. Hearing that Victoria was about to pay a visit, the minister had Towser banished from the church. The Queen was disappointed, and told the minister so. She had seen a sketch of the church interior with the dog in his usual place and had wanted to meet him. Towser was allowed to remain in future. The Court Circulars often mentioned canine visitors as well. Frequently, they were brought to court at the Queen's command.

Like many of her colleagues, Emma had her own dog, a fox terrier named Chat. Obviously a spoiled darling, the dog would not eat a large piece of cake or biscuit, ignoring it unless it was broken up. The Queen, of course, fussed over the little dog whenever she visited. On one occasion, she offered Chat a biscuit. It was unbroken, and Emma panicked.

"I was in fear and trembling, as I believed I knew what would happen. Chat, however, seemed to know that she must behave, and she took the biscuit and ate it without more ado, much to my relief."[15]

Near Braemar was a Catholic church, and Emma sang there on one occasion for the benefit of the parishioners. She had a social life too, often lunching at Lord Fife's. One year, she met and sang for Prime Minister William Gladstone and his wife. Later, the Gladstones and their host called on Emma for tea, and Emma "had the pleasure of a long conversation with Mr. Gladstone. His personality charmed me and I was particularly impressed by his great interest in music and by the beautiful quality of his speaking voice."[16] Emma apparently did not share the Queen's dislike of Gladstone; she even obtained his autograph for her autograph book.

One of Victoria's favourite amusements in the Highlands was the gillies' ball. Although members of her family disliked the balls, which often deteriorated into drunken free-for-alls, the Queen felt the noise and rowdyism gave her Scottish servants an opportunity to celebrate without the strictures of royal etiquette. She always attended, and often invited others along. So Emma and her sister Cornélia both went to one gillies' ball and stayed up until early morning, dancing and undoubtedly singing with the other revellers.

As a ruling sovereign, Victoria never had any very close friendships with other women. She did not make friends easily, for she was extremely shy and lacked confidence. Yet many people who met her found her a gracious lady with kindly blue eyes and a knack for putting people at ease.

How close was the friendship between Victoria and Emma? There was mutual respect. Emma, as a staunch monarchist, greatly admired the Queen. Victoria, in her turn, appreciated Emma's talent and accomplishments. There were vast differences in age, education and social status, but they shared a passionate love of music, and similar outlooks on morality and respectability. Also they both liked animals, and they knew many of the same people.

Throughout their association, the Queen frequently presented Emma with gifts. Among these were two portraits, one taken at Victoria's accession, and a second taking during her silver jubilee. On another occasion, she presented Emma with another picture in a silver and enamel case, saying, "I hear that you always carry my photograph with you in your travels. This one will be a more convenient one."[17] Like the pearl cross and necklace Victoria had given her, Emma cherished the miniature portrait throughout her life.

Perhaps the best indication of Victoria's respect for Emma, both as a singer and as a person, was her funeral arrangements. The Queen had written detailed instructions; for the private family funeral service the great Albani was requested to sing for her sovereign one last time.

Victoria's death came at the end of an era of much peace and prosperity for England and the world. When the Queen died on 22 January 1901, many people around the globe lived under British law, and millions more were ruled by Victoria's descendants and relatives. Soon World War I would put an end to a way of life that had endured for generations. There were few indications among these in Victoria's death chamber at Windsor Castle, that Europe was heading for a major conflict. Her grandson, Kaiser Wilhelm of Germany, was there with her sons and daughters, and they all assisted in the funeral preparations.

Victorians were obsessed by death. Hair wreaths, funerary jewellery, crepe and widow's weeds were everywhere, with mourning often carried to ridiculous extremes. While Victoria was no stranger to death — she had lost her beloved Albert as well as some of her children and grandchildren — she did not believe it necessarily meant darkness. For example, it would mean reunion with Albert. So, while she understood the need for personal mourning, she was completely opposed to the ostentatious funeral trappings so commonplace in her realm. Determined to get things her own way one last time, she planned her funeral in careful detail.

No undertakers with their sombre dress and unctuous expressions would be allowed, and her funeral would be as simple as possible considering her station. She had been impressed by the simplicity of Prince Leopold's and Prince Henry's military funerals, as well as by the white embroidered pall which covered Alfred, Lord Tennyson's coffin. At one point, she even expressed a wish that all funerals could be white, and as much as possible she tried to make her own funeral a white one. She was dressed in white, with a white cap on her head, and was lifted gently into her coffin by the new King Edward and his brother. The silver cross which had hung on the wall above her bed was taken down and placed in her hands. Then her wedding veil was drawn over her face and spring flowers sprinkled over her body and the casket.

While her subjects mourned Victoria's body lay in state at Osborne House for ten days. In early February, the casket was placed aboard the royal yacht *Alberta* and transported to the mainland, then carried by train to London. For a little while longer she rested in the Albert Memorial Chapel, until the funeral services took place.

After the pomp of an official state funeral, Victoria's family must have welcomed the privacy of the final services on the evening of 3 February. Dressed in black, the women's faces covered by veils, the family gathered at St. George's

Chapel. In the dimly lit room, Emma sang for her Queen one last time; excerpts from Handel's *Messiah*, and the hymns, *Come unto him* and *I know that my Redeemer liveth*. As the family rose to follow the casket to the mausoleum Victoria had built as Albert's and her own final resting place, King Edward thanked her with tears in his eyes.

"It was a terribly hard task," Emma later recalled, "but the memory of the dear Queen and all of her goodness to me gave me courage."[18]

Emma could not have known then, but with Victoria's passing her own career was almost at an end. Barring accident, serious illness or complete retirement, a career does not end quite as abruptly as life, but there were indications that Emma's voice was deteriorating. Operatic performances were a part of the past for her, and, as in her early years, she returned to giving concerts, travelling widely, singing before audiences throughout the world. Although she was in her mid-fifties, her energy level remained high. In 1906 she undertook an extensive farewell tour of Canada, travelling from coast to coast to sing and marvel at the scenery. This time she had her own troupe with her, and among them was Eva Gauthier, an Ottawa-born mezzo-soprnano whom Emma had taken under her wing. At one point, Emma announced, "As an artistic legacy to my country, I leave you Eva Gauthier."[19]

Although her audiences were still warmly receptive, Emma realized it was time to retire and on 14 October 1911 she gave her last public recital. Adelina Patti and Nellie Melba were among the supporting artists, and the audience was deeply moved by the Canadian singer's final performance. The following month, Emma published her autobiography.

Forty Years of Song recounts many pleasant memories of Emma's long and successful career. There are few criticisms of any of her colleagues, for Emma seems to have followed the rule "if you can't say anything nice, don't say anything." The overall impression the book creates is that of a dedicated professional who has been richly rewarded for her hard work and is now prepared to enjoy her last years in gracious retirement.

But the fates which had been kind to Emma Albani throughout her life, now turned away from her. Instead of peaceful respite, her retirement brought more heartache and sorrow than she had experienced since childhood.

Photographs of performers often appeared on music which they had helped to make popular. This is one of the songs that Emma Albani sang at Queen Victoria's funeral.

Chapter Nineteen

The Final Act

"A prima donna dies three deaths: when her beauty fades, when her voice fails, and when the breath leaves her body," Lillian Nordica once observed.[1] Ten years Emma's junior, Nordica died in 1914 on Java following a shipwreck and so never experienced that fourth kind of death — poverty.

Never truly beautiful, Emma had learned to improve her natural looks with the help of curling irons and paint. Her voice never really failed her, only gradually deteriorated. But both occurrences were quite predictable, and, if not welcome, were accepted as part of the natural order of things. What neither Ernest nor Emma could have forseen, however, was the financial difficulty they encountered following World War I. They had both made fortunes, but financial reverses, the high cost of living, and the pressure of the society which expected them to keep lavish living styles eroded their savings. Instead of living out her retirement in comfort, Emma was forced to sing in music halls and to take in pupils.

Yet the interlude in music halls was brief, as Emma was simply too old for regular stage appearances, and the audiences who frequented the music halls were unlike those who had attended her concerts or operas. Teaching was a more acceptable alternative, so Emma sent out notices announcing her availability as a teacher. In classes or private sessions she would instruct pupils in singing, voice culture and the art of breathing, emphasizing, of course, the old Italian method she herself had mastered. Twelve private lessons cost eight pounds, and the notice stipulated the first six lessons should be paid in advance.

The lessons did not quite earn enough money to meet expenses, nor did the sale of many of Emma's treasured souvenirs of her performances for royalty. Eventually, Emma had to rent her home at Tregunter Road in Kensington and lease a smaller place. In 1920 after some of Emma's influential friends drew attention to her plight and also to the embarass-

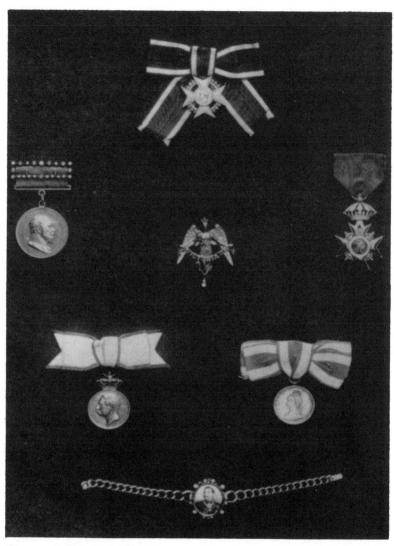

Some of Emma Albani's medals and decorations that she received from fans who were heads of state.

ment of having a famous prima donna and former favourite of Queen Victoria living close to poverty, the British government voted her a yearly allowance of £100. In contrast, this was a small token of appreciation, for Emma had been showered with jewels, titles and honours throughout her career. The Royal Order of Kapiolani was bestowed on her by King Kalakaua of Hawaii in the early 1890s. In 1897 she won the Royal Philharmonic Society's Beethoven Medal, an honour given in previous years to Gounod, Brahms and Adelina Patti. In 1925 when it appeared she had been all but forgotten, Emma was made Dame Commander of the British Empire by King George V. Ernest was made Knight Commander of the Order at the same time, more as a consequence of Emma's reflected glory than his own achievements.

The Most Excellent Order of the British Empire had been created in June 1917 to reward civilians of the Empire who rendered special services. Scores were honoured yearly, so Emma and Ernest would have been only two of many to receive the Order at Buckingham Palace. As Emma climbed the dais to receive the badge on its purple ribbon and shake the hand of the king, it would have been difficult for her not to recall the many ruling monarchs she had met before. Most were dead; many of their thrones were now part of the past. But, in the crowded palace room, Emma must have re-experienced, if only for a moment, the feeling of sweet triumph so familiar in former days.

Unfortunately, such honours did little to help solve her financial problems. Yet Emma remained more than willing to help others. She used her influence to advance the career of Eva Gauthier, writing to anyone she thought could help her. When another friend wrote a biography of Sarah Bernhardt, Emma wrote a letter to the editor of the *Montreal Gazette* asking him to help promote that book.

In 1924, Canadian prime minister William Lyon Mackenzie King travelled to London and called on Canada's most famous singer. He was horrified at what he found. Emma had become "old, and feeble, and dependent ... married to an old man named Gye who is quite as helpless as herself."[2] Among other topics, Emma and King must have talked about Sir Wilfrid Laurier, King's mentor, who Emma greatly admired. By the time he left London, King's crusading spirit was aroused. He was determined to do something to improve Emma's situation.

Before Parliament prorogued that summer, King attempted to have the government provide a pension for Emma. He might have succeeded with a majority government, but he did not possess a majority in the House of Commons. In writing to Emma to explain the situation that August, King held out the hope that perhaps the Quebec government would be able to provide some assistance, adding, "I appreciate of course that you belong to Canada rather than to a province; when I urged this point I met with the reprimand that you belonged also to the world and more particularly to the British Isles with which your professional life and present days are so intimately associated."[3] He ended the letter with a promise to continue to try to find a way to help her.

King wrote to Ernest Lapointe, a member of Parliament, asking him to speak to Quebec provincial premier Taschereau on the subject. Pointing out that Emma was already very old and unlikely to live much longer, King said, "it would I think be a misfortune ... if she were obliged to end her days in penury, wholly dependent, as she now is, on private philanthropy. Her career has been too splendidly associated with the name of our country to let it suffer this kind of eclipse."[4] The Quebec government was unimpressed and, like the federal government, took no steps to help Emma.

Early in March 1925, King wrote to Lord Atholstan of the *Montreal Star* asking him to institute a newspaper subscription campaign, a fund-raising drive to ease Emma's difficulty. Atholstan refused, telling King that the subscription technique had been overdone and that, having given so much to other causes, generous *Star* readers were "feeling poorly just now."[5]

Meanwhile, there was an active movement in England to raise money for Emma. With Ernest's death in 1925 she was in more serious financial need than ever. At seventy-seven she could hardly be expected to work for a living, and, although her son helped out when he could, there was never enough money to meet her needs. King was approached with a request to be a patron of the English fund-raising drive, but he refused. If anything could be done to rouse Canadians from their apathy, he pointed out, he would be obliged to support whatever steps his countrymen took.

Finally, *La Presse*, Montreal's French language daily newspaper, organized a subscription and a benefit concert. Under the patronage of the King of England, it was called "hommage national à Albani." In a series of front page articles, the newspaper outlined the reason for the fund, advertised the benefit concert, and published the names of donors. *La Presse* based its appeal on nationalist sentiment, after all, Emma was a Canadian. What a shame it would be if Canadians, especially French-Canadians, ignored her plight when so many other citizens of the British Commonwealth were rallying to her aid. The concert took place was at the Théâtre St.-Denis in Montreal on 28 May 1925, and various notables were among the patrons of the event, including Mackenzie King, the president of the CPR, Senator Dandurand, and the French Consul-General.

The London benefit concert had been held on 25 May with Nellie Melba as the star of the show, supported by Edward Elgar and Sir Henry Wood. Sarah Fischer, another of Emma's protegées, also took part. When Melba led her out onto the stage to face the audience, Emma was so overcome with emotion she could not speak.

Inspired by the London concert's success, the citizens of Emma's hometown requested permission to use old Fort Chambly as the setting for a benefit concert, also under the auspices of *La Presse*. Permission was granted by the National Parks Commission as Fort Chambly is a national historic site and the concert was scheduled for the beginning of June. Tickets sold for 50¢ each. Those who attended were almost immediately aware of the photograph of Emma, surrounded by the flags of England, France and the United States, which decorated the stage. In addition to instrumental music and singing, there were various speeches honouring Emma and drawing attention to the sad reversal of her fortunes.

All in all, the belated efforts on Emma's behalf were successful. The *La Presse* subscription and benefit concerts netted $4,095.55. Emma was able to return to her Kensington home and live in comfort.

To have lost one's beauty, fortune, voice and one's husband were tragedy enough. For Emma the widespread fundraising efforts on her behalf must have been another kind of difficulty, a humiliating experience for a woman who had associated with royalty and earned more money than many of her fans could ever imagine. Emma accepted th world's charity as best she could, but there was a hint of her pain in the comment she made. "I believed that my country had forgotten me, I who never forgot it. It is so touching to know that on the other side of the great Atlantic ocean I am thought of."[6]

Emma survived for nearly five years after the benefit concerts. On 3 April 1930 she died peacefully at her home. Two days later, her funeral procession, including her son and the Canadian High Commissioner to Britain, left the nearby Servite Church for Brompton Cemetery in London where Emma was buried beside Ernest.

Afterword

Emma's death caused some interest in many of the places she had lived or visited, but it quickly subsided. Absorbed in the hardships of the Depression or the amusement of radio and movies, most Canadians, Europeans, and Americans had little time to think about a singer whose last operatic performance had been in 1896. Emma was rapidly forgotten by all but serious students of music.

Outside of French Canada, she is hardly known today. There is a plaque in her honour in Chambly, a street named after her in Montreal. The Chambly historical society does much to keep her memory alive, as does Gilles Potvin, an editor of the *Encyclopedia of Music in Canada* and translator of *Forty Years of Song*. An oil painting and bust of Emma are in the collection of the Musée de Québec in Quebec City, and in 1980 Canada Post issued a stamp commemorating the fiftieth anniversary of her death.

Her bachelor son, Frederick-Ernest Gye, had a fine diplomatic career, then lived in Montreal from 1941 to 1952, but died in London in 1955. In 1934, after his mother's death, Frederick funded the Albani prize at London's Royal Conservatory of Music to be awarded annually to a young singer.

Still, most Canadians have never heard of her. Ask the average Canadian who our first international opera star was and you will probably get the reply: Maureen Forrester. Yet Forrester is, in a way, a musical descendant of Emma's, for her debut in Montreal took place at a Sarah Fischer concert, as did the debuts of composers André Prevost and Violet Archer. These Sarah Fischer Concert scholarships in memory of Emma to help aspiring young Canadian musicians were instituted by Miss Fischer in 1946.

But Emma's contribution to Canada's national heritage goes far beyond the confines of the musical world. While Canada was still little more than a frontier country, she proved that its citizens could compete with the finest professionals of other countries, could match and often surpass them.

Chronology

1847 November 1, Born Emma Lajeunesse in Chambly, Lower Canada (Quebec)

1849 May 31, Sister, Cornélia Lajeunesse born

1850 August 19, Brother, Joseph-Adélard Lajeunesse born

1856 March 26, Mélina Mignault Lajeunesse, her mother, dies
September 19, First concert, Montreal

1858 September 9, Enters Sacré-Coeur convent, Sault-au-Récollet

1859 June 23, First Communion

1860 August 30, Concert for HRH Prince of Wales

1861 January 29, Confirmation

1862 September 13, Fund-raising concert, Mechanics' Hall, Montreal

1864 June 16, Concert at Tweddle Hall, Albany, New York

1865 July 9, Left Sacré-Coeur convent

1868 February 25, Concert in Albany, New York
Departure for Europe
March 9, First public concert in Paris at Salle Érard

1870 April 30, Debut in Messina, Sicily, as Emma Albani, *La Sonnambula*.
Winter season in Malta (1870-71)

1871 June, Arrival in London.
Contract with Frederick Gye

1872 April 2, Covent Garden Debut, *La Sonnambula*.
September-October, First oratorio, Norwich Festival

1873 October 24, Paris debut at the Théâtre-des-Italiens, *La Sonnambula.*
Moscow (winter season)

1874 July 8, Debut at Windsor
October 21, North American operatic debut: *La Sonnambula* at New York's Academy of Music
First American tour under Strakosch
First biography by Napoléon Legendre published in Quebec City.

1875 Emma stars in London premiere of *Lohengrin* and in *Faust* at Covent Garden

1876 London premiere of *Tannhäuser*, Emma as Elisabeth

1877 Emma appears in the Handel Festival at the Crystal Palace.

1878 June 1, Emma sings Virginia in *Paul et Virginie*
August 6, Marries Ernest Gye, son of Frederick Gye.
December 4, Frederick Gye dies after hunting accident

1879 June 4, Emma's only child, Frederick-Ernest, born.

1880 Lead female role in Arthur Sullivan's *Martyr of Antioch*

1881 Fiasco at La Scala when Emma appears in *Lucia di Lammermoor* and *Rigoletto*

1882 After performing *Lohengrin* in Berlin, is made Hofkammersängerin by Kaiser Wilhelm

1883 January 15, Albany Music Hall
February 23, White House performance
Second North American tour including Canada
March 29, Return for visit to Sacré-Coeur

1884 Tours in Belgium, Holland
Last Gye season at Covent Garden

1885 Première of Gounod's *Mors et Vita*, Leeds Festival

1886 Emma sings lead in *St. Elizabeth* for Liszt on his farewell visit to England.

1888 Appearances in Denmark

1889 October 9, Harmanus Bleeker Hall, Albany
Canadian Tour
American Tour under Grau and Abbey, including visit to
Mexico.

1890 March 24, Emma is first Desdemona at Metropolitan Opera,
New York.
April 24-26, Appearances in Albany.

1891 December 23, Debut as Metropolitan Opera's leading soprano
for 1891-92 season, as Gilda in *Rigoletto*

1892 March 31, Emma's performance as Senta in *The Flying Dutchman* ends her only full Metropolitan season and marks her last
operatic performance in the United States.

1893 German performances

1896 February 4, Public reception at Albany Club for Emma
June 26, Isolde with Jean de Reszke as Tristan at Covent
Garden — considered the finest performances of her career
July 23, *Don Giovanni* at Covent Garden (Donna Anna)
July 24, *Les Huguenots*. Emma's last Covent Garden role (Val-
entine), last operatic performance anywhere.

1897 Emma awarded Beethoven Medal by Royal Philharmonic
Society

1898 Concert tours in Austria, Australia, South Africa.

1901 January, Death of Queen Victoria, Emma sings at family
funeral.
November 14, Henry Mapleson dies
Tours of Canada, United States, Australia, South Africa, New
Zealand

1902 August 9, Emma sings at coronation of King Edward VII

1903 Canadian Tour

1904 August 2, Joseph Lajeunesse buried in Chambly
Between 1904-07 Emma made some recordings

1906 Canadian "farewell tour"

1907 Ceylon and India

1911 October 14, London farewell performance with Patti and Melba at Albert Hall.
Autobiography, *Forty Years of Song*, published

1920 British government awards Emma an annual pension of £100.

1925 Emma made Dame Commander of the British Empire (DBE)
Ernest Gye dies
May 25, Covent Garden gala concert held to raise funds for Emma.
May 28 and June 6, Similar concerts held in Montreal and Chambly.

1930 April 3, Emma dies peacefully at home
April 5, Emma buried next to Ernest at Brompton Cemetery

1938 First major biography, *L'Albani, sa carrière artistique et triomphale*, by Hélène Charbonneau, published in Montreal.

1939 Unveiling of a plaque in Chambly in presence of Emma's son

1967 Eight of Emma's recordings re-released to celebrate Canada's centennial year.

1972 French annotated translation of *Forty Years of Song* by Gilles Potvin published in Montreal as *Mémoires d'Emma Albani*

1980 Canada Post releases commemorative stamp on fiftieth anniversary of her death.

Notes

Preface

1. Emma Albani, *Forty Years of Song*, London, 1911.

Chapter One
1. Albani, p. 13
2. *Ibid.*, p. 14
3. *Ibid.*, p. 13
4. *Ibid.*, p. 15
5. *Ibid.*, p. 22

Chapter Two
1. Handbill printed for Sisters of Sacré-Coeur, Sacré-Coeur Archives.
2. Albani, p. 19
3. New York Herald, quoted by William Stephenson in *Dawn of the Nation 1860-1870*. Natural Science of Canada Limited, Toronto, 1977, p. 14.
4. Albani, p. 21
5. *Ibid.*

Chapter Three
1. Handbill quoted in *Albany Times Union*, 11 August 1940.
2. Albani, p. 25

Chapter Four
1. Henry Pleasants, *The Great Singers: From the Dawn of Opera to Our Own Time*. Simon & Schuster, New York, 1966, p. 169
2. *Ibid.*
3. *Ibid.*
4. Albani, p. 30
5. *Ibid.*, p. 28
6. *Ibid.*, p. 27

Chapter Five
1. Albani, p. 33
2. *Ibid.*, p. 35
3. *Ibid.*, p. 38
4. Pleasants, p. 198
5. Albani, p. 50

Chapter Six
1. James Henry Mapleson, *The Mapleson Memoirs*, Clarke & Compon, New York, 1888. Volume I, p. 141.
2. *Ibid.*, p. 142
3. Albani Collection, National Library of Canada.
4. Albani, p. 66.
5. *Ibid.*, p. 67.

Chapter Seven
1. Albani, p. 68
2. Clara Louise Kellogg, *Memoirs of an American Prima Donna*, G. Putnam's Songs, New York, 1913. pp. 179-180.
3. *Ibid.* p. 180.
4. David Bispham, *A Quaker Singer's Recollections*, Macmillan Company, New York, 1921, p. 61.
5. Albani, pp 69-70.
6. *Ibid.*, p. 76.
7. Kellogg, p. 130
8. Henry Finck, *My Adventures in the Golden Age of Music*, Funk & Wagnalls, New York, 1926. p. 184.
9. Albani, p. 77

Chapter Eight
1. Kellogg, p. 317.
2. Ira Glackens, *Yankee Diva*, Coleridge Press, New York, 1963, p. 75.
3. Albani, p. 80.
4. Elizabeth Longford, *Victoria R.I.*, Weidenfeld & Nicolson, London, 1964, p. 394.
5. *Ibid.*, p. 393.
6. *Ibid.*, p. 394.
7. Albani, p. 86.
8. *Ibid.*, p. 85.

Chapter Nine
1. *New York Herald*, 24 October 1874, quoted by Albani, p. 98.
2. *Albany Argus*, ? November 1874.
3. Albani, pp. 101-2.
4. *Albany Morning Express*, quoted by Albani, p. 103.
5. Mapleson, Volume 2, p. 18.

Chapter Ten
1. Albani, p. 127.
2. *Ibid.*, p. 140.
3. *Ibid.*, p. 131.
4. *Ibid.*, p. 132.
5. *Ibid.*, p. 135.
6. Helmut Kallman *et al. Encyclopedia of Music in Canada.* University of Toronto Press, Toronto, 1981, p. 11.
7. Albani, p. 136.
8. *Ibid.*
9. Christopher Hibbert, *Gilbert and Sullivan and their Victorian World*, American Heritage Publishing Company, New York, 1976, p. 192.
10. *Leeds Mercury* quoted by Hibbert, pp. 193.
11. *Ibid.*, 192-3.
12. Caryl Brahms, *Lost Chords and Discords*, Weidenfeld & Nicolson, London, 1975, p. 171.
13. Hermann Klein, *Great Woman Singers of My Time*, G. Routledge and Company, 1931, p. 110.

Chapter Eleven
1. Mapleson, Volume I, p. 298.
2. *Ibid.*, pp. 302-3.
3. *Albany Journal*, 16 January 1883.

4. Albani, p. 172.
5. Mapleson, Volume I, p. 305.
6. *Ibid.*, p. 310.
7. *Ibid.*, p. 311.
8. *The Globe*, 14 February 1883.
9. Albani, pp. 172-3.
10. *Ibid.*, p. 175.
11. *Ibid.*, p. 180.
12. *Ibid.*, p. 182.
13. *Ibid.*, pp. 182-3.
14. Journal, Archives of the Convent of the Sacred Heart.

Chapter Twelve
1. Hermann Klein, *Thirty Years of Musical Life in London*, The Century Company, New York, 1903. p. 67.
2. Mapleson, Volume II, pp. 172-3.
3. Finck, p. 184.
4. Klein, *Great Women Singers of My Time*, p. 107.
5. Albani, p. 60.
6. Oscar Thompson, *The American Singer*, The Dial Press, New York, 1937, p. 155.
7. Finck, p. 123.
8. Clara Leiser, *Jean de Reszke and the Great Days of Opera*, Minton, Balch & Company, 1934. p. 203.
9. George Bernard Shaw, *London Music in 1888-1889, as heard by Corno di Bassetto (later known as Bernard Shaw)*, Dodd, Mead & Company, New York, 1937.
10. Klein, *The Golden Age of Opera*, p. 196.
11. Leiser, p. 246.
12. Klein, *Thirty Years of Musical Life in London*

Chapter Thirteen
1. Shaw, pp. 53-4.
2. Bispham, pp. 169-170.
3. Agnes G. Murphy, *Melba*. Doubleday, New York, 1909. p. 112.
4. Shaw, pp. 49-50.
5. *Ibid.*, p. 52.
6. *Ibid.*, p. 140.
7. Thompson, p. 158.
8. Kallman, p. 11.
9. Alec Robertson, *Dvorak*. J.M. Dent & Sons, London, 1964, p. 54.
10. Albani, p. 75.
11. *Ibid.*
12. *Ibid.*, pp. 129-130.
13. *The Canadian Magazine*. March 1903.

Chapter Fourteen
1. *The Spectator*, 13 February, 1889.
2. Albani, p. 212.
3. *The Spectator*, 13 February 1889.
4. Albani, p. 213.
5. Reported in *The Spectator*, 14 February 1889.
6. *The Spectator*, 13 February 1889.
7. Albani, p. 217.

Chapter Fifteen
1. Albani, p. 220.
2. Luigi Arditi, *My Reminiscences*. Dodd, Mead & Company, New York, 1896. p. 235.
3. *Ibid.*, p. 211.
4. Mapleson, Volume II, p. 217.
5. Arditi, p. 239.
6. *Ibid.*, p. 236.
7. *Ibid.*, p. 233.
8. *Ibid.*, p. 239.
9. Ronald Davis, *Opera in Chicago*, Appleton-Century, 1966, p. 51.
10. Albani, p. 219.
11. *Ibid.*
12. Arditi, p. 240.

Chapter Sixteen
1. Albani, p. 224.
2. *Ibid.*, p. 222.
3. Arditi, p. 248.
4. Albani, p. 223.
5. *Ibid.*, p. 225.
6. George C. Odell, *Annals of the New York Stage*, Columbia University Press, Volume XIV, 1889-90.
7. Leiser, p. 197.
8. *Albany Evening Journal*, April 26, 1890.
9. William Henry Drummond, *The Poetical Works of William Henry Drummond*, McClelland and Stewart, Toronto, 1926.
10. Quaintance Eaton, *Opera Caravan: Adventures of the Metropolitan 1883-1956*. Da Capo Press, 1957, p. 45.

Chapter Seventeen
1. Irving Kolodin, *The Metropolitan Opera 1883-1966, A Candid History*. Alfred A. Knopf, 1966. p. XX
2. Leiser, p. 118.
3. Albani, p. 232.
4. *Ibid.*, p. 238.
5. Letter from Adam Brown, 21 March 1896, to his wife in Hamilton Public Library's Brown-Hendrie Collection.
6. *The Spectator*, 23 March 1896.
7. Albani, p. 267.
8. *Ibid.*, p. 269.
9. *Ibid.*, p. 270.
10. Ariditi, p. 239.
11. *The Strand Magazine*, Illustrated Interviews, No. III, Madame Albani. 1900.
12. Albani, p. 275.

Chapter Eighteen
1. Alan Hardy, *Queen Victoria Was Amused*, Taplinger Publishing Company, New York, 1976. p. 21.
2. *Ibid.*, p. 52.
3. Albani, p. 91.
4. *Ibid.*, p. 92.
5. *Ibid.*, p. 93.
6. Hardy, p. 160.

7. Leiser, p. 75.
8. *Ibid.*, p. 76.
9. Hardy, p. 161.
10. Albani, p. 185.
11. *Ibid.*, p. 186.
12. *Ibid.*, pp. 186-7.
13. *Ibid.*, pp. 117.
14. Hardy, p. 56.
15. Albani, p. 188.
16. *Ibid.*, p. 190.
17. *Ibid.*, p. 94.
18. *The Canadian Magazine*, January 1912.
19. Helmut Kallmann *et al., Encyclopedia of Music in Canada*, University of Toronto Press, 1981, p. 369.

Chapter Nineteen
1. Glackens, p. 255.
2. Albani Collection, National Library of Canada.
3. *Ibid.*
4. *Ibid.*
5. *Ibid.*
6. "L'hommage national à Albani" in *Les Cahiers de la Seigneurie de Chambly*, Volume 2, Number 1, February 1980, p. 42.

General Bibliography

Albani, Emma. *Forty Years of Song.* London: Mills & Boon, Ltd., 1911.

Arditi, Luigi. *My Reminiscences.* New York: Dodd, Mead & Co., 1896.

Armstrong, William. *The Romantic World of Music.* New York: E.P. Dutton, 1922.

Benson, E.F. *As We Were: A Victorian Peep-Show.* London: Longmans, Green and Company, 1930.

Bettman, Otto L. *The Good Old Days — They Were Terrible!* New York: Random House, 1974.

Bispham, David. *A Quaker Singer's Recollections.* New York: The Macmillan Company, 1921.

Brahms, Caryl. *Gilbert and Sullivan: Lost Chords and Discords.* London: Weidenfeld and Nicolson, 1975.

Brinin, John Malcolm. *The Sway of the Grand Saloon.* New York: Delacorte Press, 1971.

Buffin, F.F. *Musical Celebrities.* London, 1938.

Bulman, Joan. *Jenny Lind.* London: James Barrie Publishers, 1956.

Burchell, S.C. *Age of Progress.* New York: Time-Life Books, 1966.

Carroll, Joy. *Pioneer Days: 1840-1860.* Toronto: Natural Science of Canada Limited, 1979.

Charbonneau, Hélène. *L'Albani, sa carrière artistique et triomphale.* Montreal: Imprimerie Jacques-Cartier, 1938.

Damrosch, Walter. *My Musical Life.* New York: Charles Scribner's Sons, 1923.

Davis, Ronald. *Opera in Chicago — A Social and Cultural History, 1850-1965.* New York: Appleton-Century Press, 1966.

Drummond, W.H. *The Poetical Works of William Henry Drummond.* Toronto: McClelland & Stewart, 1926.

Duprez, Gilbert-Louis. *Souvenirs d'un Chanteur.* Paris: 1888.

Eames, Emma. *Some Memories and Reflections.* New York, 1927.

Eaton, Quaintance. *Opera Caravan: Adventures of the Metropolitan 1883-1956.* New York: Da Capo Press, 1957.

Finck, Henry T. *My Adventures in the Golden Age of Music.* New York: Funk & Wagnalls, 1926.

Glackens, Ira. *Yankee Diva: Lillian Nordica and the Golden Days of Opera.* New York: Coleridge Press, 1963.

Grout, Donald Jay. *A History of Western Music.* Third Edition, W.W. Norton & Company, Inc., 1980.

Guernsey, Betty. *Gaby: The Life and Times of Gaby Bernier, Couturière Extraordinaire.* Toronto: The Maincourt Press, 1982.

Hardy, Alan. *Queen Victoria Was Amused.* New York: Taplinger Publishing Company, 1976.

Hauk, Minnie. *Memories of a Singer.* London: 1925.

Hibbert, Christopher. *Gilbert and Sullivan and their Victorian World.* New York: American Heritage Publishing Co., Inc. 1976.

Houden, N.J., editor. *Catholic Albany.* Albany: Peter Donnelly, 1895.

Howell & Tenney. *History of the County of Albany, N.Y., from 1609 to 1886.* New York: W.W. Munsell & Co., 1886.

Hughes, Spike. *Great Opera Houses.* London: Weidenfeld & Nicolson, 1956.

Jenkins, Kathleen. *Montreal, Island City of the St. Lawrence.* New York: Doubleday & Company, 1966.

Kallmann, Helmut. *A History of Music in Canada 1534-1914.* Toronto: University of Toronto Press, 1960.

——————————, Gilles Potvin and Kenneth Winters, editors. *Encyclopedia of Music in Canada.* Toronto: University of Toronto Press, 1981.

Kellogg, Clara Louise. *Memoirs of an American Prima Donna.* New York: G.P. Putnam's Songs, 1913.

Klein, Hermann. *The Golden Age of Opera.* London, 1933.

——————————. *Great Women Singers of My Time.* London: G. Routledge & Company, 1931.

——————————. *The Reign of Patti.* London: 1920.

——————————. *Thirty Years of Musical Life in London, 1870-1900.* New York: The Century Company, 1903.

——————————. *Unmusical New York.* London: 1910.

Kobbé, Gustav. *Opera Singers.* Boston: Oliver Ditson Co., 1904.

Kolodin, Irving. *The Metropolitan Opera, 1883-1966, A Candid History.* New York: Alfred A. Knopf, 1966.

Krehbiel, H.E. *Chapters of Opera.* New York: Henry Holt & Company, 1908.

Lahee, Henry C. *Famous Singers of Today and Yesterday.* Boston: L.C. Page and Company, 1898.

Lavignac, Albert. *The Music Drama of Richard Wagner, and His Festival Theatre in Bayreuth.* New York: Dodd, Mead and Company, 1898.

Lawton, Mary. *Schumann-Heink, The Last of the Titans.* New York: The Macmillan Company, 1928.

Legendre, Napoléon. *Albani, Emma Lajeunesse.* Quebec: Imprimerie A. Côté et Cie, 1874.

Leiser, Clara. *Jean de Reszke and the Great Days of Opera.* Minton, Balch & Company, 1934.

Longford, Elizabeth. *Victoria, R.I.* London: Weidenfeld & Nicolson, 1964.

Mapleson, James Henry. *The Mapleson Memoirs* (2 volumes). New York: Belford, Clarke & Company, 1888.

Melba, Nellie. *Melodies and Memories.* 1925.

Murphy, Agnes. *Melba.* New York: Doubleday & Company, 1909.

Odell, George C.D. *Annals of the New York Stage.* New York: Columbia University Press, 1945.

Pearson, Hesketh. *Gilbert and Sullivan.* London: Hamish Hamilton, 1935.

Pleasants, Henry. *The Great Singers: from the Dawn of Opera to our Own Time.* New York: Simon & Schuster, 1966.

Pipes, Richard. *Russia under the Old Regime.* London: Weidenfeld & Nicolson, 1974.

Robertson, Alec. *Dvorak.* London: J.M. Dent & Sons Ltd., 1974.

Rogers, Francis. *Some Famous Singers of the Nineteenth Century.* New York: 1914.

Ryan, Thomas. *Recollections of an Old Musician.* New York: E.P. Dutton, 1899.

Seltsam, William M. (compiler). *Metropolitan Opera Annals.* New York: The H.W. Wilson Company, 1947.

Shaw, Bernard. *London Music in 1888-1889, as heard by Corno di Bassetto, (later known as Bernard Shaw).* New York: Dodd, Mead & Company, 1937.

Stephenson, William. *Dawn of the Nation, 1860-1870.* Toronto: Natural Science of Canada Limited, 1977.

Thompson, Oscar. *The American Singer — A Hundred Years of Success in Opera.* New York: The Dial Press, Inc. 1937.

Victoria, Queen. *The Letters of Queen Victoria, A Selection of Her Majesty's Correspondence*. London: John Murray, 1907-32.
_____. *Further Letters*. London: Thornton Butterworth, 1938.
Victoria, Queen. *Dearest Child: Letters between Queen Victoria and the Princess Royal*. London: Evans Brothers, 1964.

Periodicals

Clément, Marie-Blanche. "Albani" in *Le Bulletin des recherches historiques*, vol. 55, nos 10, 11, 12 (oct., nov., déc. 1949), p. 199-210.
David, L.-O. "Emma Lajeunesse" in *L'Opinion publique*, 23 avril 1870. *Mes contemporains*, Montreal, 1894.
Gagnon, Maurice. "La Diva de Chambly" in *La Patrie du dimanche*, Montreal, 9 octobre 1960.
Gilberte. "cinq minutes avec notre diva" in *Le Journal de Françoise*, Montreal, 7 février 1903.
Hale, Katherine. "Canadian Celebrities: XLI — Madame Albani." in *The Canadian Magazine*, March 1903.
How, Harry. "Illustrated Interviews: No. III — Madame Albani." in *The Strand Magazine?* 1900
Huard, Renée-C. "L'hommage national à Albani" in *Les cahiers de la seigneurie de Chambly*, Volume 2, No. 1, February 1980. Société d'histoire de la seigneurie de Chambly.
Massicotte, Edouard-Zotique, "La famille d'Albani" in *Le Bulletin des recherches historiques*, Montreal, XXXVII 11 (novembre 1931) pp., 660-669; XXXVII 12 (décembre 1931) p. 713.
Maurault, Olivier, "Albani" in *La Musique*, Quebec I, 6 (juin 1919); I, 7 (juillet 1919); I, 8 (août 1919), I, 9 (septembre 1919). "Albani, la femme, l'artiste, la Canadienne" in *La Lyre*, Montreal, avril-mai 1925.
Rivet, Marcel. "Albani, sa famille, sa paroisse." in *Les cahiers de la seigneurie de Chambly*, Volume 2, No. 2, September 1980. Société d'histoire de la seigneurie de Chambly.
Weaver, Emily. "Pioneer Canadian Women: Madame Albani." in *The Canadian Magazine*, January 1912.

Newspapers

Albany Evening Journal.	February 18, 1868
Ibid.	January 16, 1883.
Ibid.	October 10, 1889.
Ibid.	April 24, 1890.
Ibid.	April 25, 1890.
Ibid.	April 26, 1890.
Ibid.	January 30, 1892.
Ibid.	February 5, 1896.
Albany Times-Union.	August 11, 1940.
The Gazette (Montreal).	August 28, 1860.
Ibid.	March 24, 1883.
Ibid.	March 28, 1883.
Ibid.	April 1, 1883.
Ibid.	January 22, 1889.
Ibid.	January 24, 1889.
Ibid.	January 25, 1889.
Ibid.	January 26, 1889.
Ibid.	January 28, 1889.

The New York Times.	May 21, 1967.
The Plattsburgh Press-Republican.	August 12, 1940.
Ibid.	March 31, 1955.
The Plattsburgh Sentinel.	January 25, 1889.
The (Hamilton) Spectator.	February 13, 1889.
Ibid.	February 14, 1889.
Ibid.	March 23, 1896.
Ibid.	February 4, 1901.

Unpublished Sources

Brown-Hendrie Collection, Special Collections, Hamilton Public Library.
Albani Collection, National Library of Canada, Ottawa.
Personal correspondence with Sisters Annette Archambault and Annette Déry, Convent of the Sacred Heart, Montreal.

Illustration and Photography Credits

Page 04 L11592. Public Archives of Canada
Page 12 C78125. Public Archives of Canada
Page 18 Metropolitan Toronto Library. *Forty Years of Song*
Page 22 C3294-A Public Archives of Canada
Page 37 L8711. Public Archives of Canada
Page 45 Metropolitan Toronto Library. *Forty Years of Song*
Page 50 PA74126. Public Archives of Canada
Page 56 Metropolitan Toronto Library. *Illustrated London News*, 15 May 1858
Page 59 Metropolitan Toronto Library. *Forty Years of Song*
Page 66 Metropolitan Toronto Library. picture file
Page 74 Metropolitan Toronto Library. James Cammer & La Scala Autographs
Page 76 Metropolitan Toronto Library. Robert Commally
Page 97 Metropolitan Toronto Library. *Forty Years of Song*
Page 99 Metropolitan Toronto Library. German lithograph
Page 120 Metropolitan Toronto Library. James Cammer & La Scala Autographs
Page 128 Metropolitan Toronto Library. *Forty Years of Song*
Page 138 Metropolitan Toronto Library. *Mapelson's Memoirs*
Page 143 Metropolitan Toronto Library. James Cammer & La Scala Autographs
Page 155 L8448. Public Archives of Canada
Page 157 Metropolitan Toronto Library. Canadian Illustrated News, 29 August 1874
Page 160 L8712. Public Archives of Canada.
Page 167 C49577. Public Archives of Canada
Page 170 C18292. Public Archives of Canada
Page 175 Metropolitan Toronto Library. *Forty Years of Song*
Page 180 L8719. Public Archives of Canada
Page 182 Metropolitan Toronto Library. *Forty Years of Song*

Index

Abbey, Henry 108, 112, 113, 139
Academy of Music 85, 104, 117
Albert Edward, King Edward VII 31-32, 68, 100, 102, 179
Alexander II, Tsar of Russia 78-80
Alfred, Duke of Edinburgh 80-81, 100
Angels, ever bright and fair 71, 111
Annie Laurie 171
Arditi, Luigi 82, 109, 140-141
Arthur, Chester 110
Auld Lang Syne 156
Ave Maria 82, 112, 163

Balmoral Castle 173-174
Barber of Seville, The 54
Benedict, Sir Julius 69, 170, 95
Betz, Franz 118
Birmingham Festival 95-96
Bluebells of Scotland, The 171
Brighton Festival 100
Bristol Festival 95
Buckingham Palace 67-69
Burke, Thomas M.A. 35, 107

Carnaval de Venise 54
Caro nome 82
Casta Diva 96
Chicago Auditorium 147
Come unto him 179
Compte Ory, Le 63
Conroy, John J. 35-36
Costa, Michael 58, 95-96
Covent Garden 57-58, 60, 63-65, 72, 77, 82, 111-112, 117, 122-123, 164

DeReszke, Edouard 119, 121, 161, 172-173
DeReszke, Jean 119, 121-122, 161-162, 172-173
Don Giovanni 161
Duprez, Gilbert-Louis 41-42, 72
Dvorak, Antonin 127

Elijah 95
Eugénie, Empress of France 40, 43

Faust 108, 151-152, 154, 161, 171
Fischer, Sarah 185, 187
Flying Dutchman, The 108, 117, 161
Fréchette, Louis-Honoré 110-111, 156
From Thy love as a Father 98

Gade, Niels 96
Gauthier, Eva 179, 183
Gladstone, William 176
God Save the Queen 165
Golden Legend, The 100-102, 171-172
Gounod, Charles 96, 98
Grand Opera House, Toronto 109
Grau, Maurice 139
Gye, Ernest 84, 87, 91-92, 112, 123, 132-135, 156, 183-184
Gye, Frederick 58, 60, 61, 63-64, 92, 93, 96
Gye, Frederick-Ernest 93, 100, 132, 176, 186-187
Gye, Herbert 104, 106

Haight, Annie 36, 107
Hamlet 72, 79
Harrison, Benjamin 146
Hauk, Minnie 89, 90, 141-142
Hear my prayer 96
Home, Sweet Home 54, 82, 106, 112, 156, 165
Huguenots, Les 147, 161
Hymn of Praise 95

I know that my Redeemer liveth 179
I Puritani 107

Joseph 92
Judas Maccabeus 35

Kellogg, Clara Louise 68, 77
King, William Lyon Mackenzie 183-185

Lajeunesse, Cornélia 23, 25, 28, 30, 33-35, 63, 92, 177
Lajeunesse, Joseph 19-20, 24-28, 30, 33, 36, 65, 92, 132, 136
Lajeunesse, Joseph-Adélard 23, 28, 29
Lajeunesse, Mélina (née Mignault) 19, 26
Laffitte, Mme Baronne de 39, 42-43
Lamperti, Francesco 44, 46-47, 52, 61, 62
La Scala 93-94
Last Rose of Summer, The 34, 54
Leeds Festival 98, 100-103
Legend of St. Elizabeth, The 127
Lind, Jenny 53, 96, 98, 169
Linda di Chamounix 67
Liverpool Festival 84
Lohengrin 116-118, 172-173
Lucia di Lammermoor 63, 67, 72, 79, 85, 91, 93, 109, 111

Mapleson, James Henry 57, 60, 61, 88, 104-105, 107-109, 113
Marriage of Figaro, The 72, 112, 166
Martha 67
Martyr of Antioch, The 98, 100
Mechanics' Hall, Montreal 25, 33, 111
Melba, Nellie 125-126, 179, 185
Meistersinger, Die 121
Messiah 94-95, 126, 179
Metropolitan Opera, New York 104, 112-113, 131, 153-154, 161-162, 164
Mignault, Mélina (see Lajeunesse, Mélina)
Mignon 61-63, 85
Mount of Olives 95
Music Hall, Albany 106

Napoleon III 39
Niemann, Albert 118
Nilsson, Christine 108, 113
Nordica, Lillian 79, 144-145, 181
Norma 96
Norwich Festival 70-71, 92, 94-95
Novello, Clara 70

Old Mar Lodge 173-176
Otello 147-148, 151, 153-154, 161-162

Patey, Janet 95
Patti, Adelina 32, 60, 69, 72-75, 81, 105, 108, 118, 124-126, 131, 145-147, 179
Pergola Theatre, Florence 61, 63
Pittman, Josiah 69-70
Pré-aux-clercs 111

Queen's Hall, Montreal 111

Ravelli, Luigi 104-105, 109, 141-142
Redemption 96
Requiem 127
Requiem Mass 127
Rigoletto 72, 79, 85, 93
Robin Adair 54, 82, 156

Sacré-Coeur Convent 29-33, 112
St. Cecilia 95
St. Ludmilla 127
Salle Ventadour 72
Shaw, George Bernard 121, 124-126

Sonnambula, La 47, 54, 64, 72, 79, 85
Souvenirs du jeune âge 111
Spectre's Bride, The 127
Strakosch, Maurice 44
Sullivan, Arthur 98, 100-103

Tamagno, Francesco 142, 147-148, 151-154
Tännhauser 117
Théâtre-des-Italiens 72
Thomas, Ambroise 61-63
Titiens, Thérèse 71, 88
Torrington, Frederick Herbert 32
Traviata, La 126, 172
Tristan und Isolde 122-123
Tweddle Hall, Albany 34-35

Victoria, Queen 57, 68, 80-83, 169-179
Von Bulow, Hans 114, 117

Wagner, Richard 23, 114-119
Windsor Castle 82, 171, 178